BEHOLD MY SERVANT

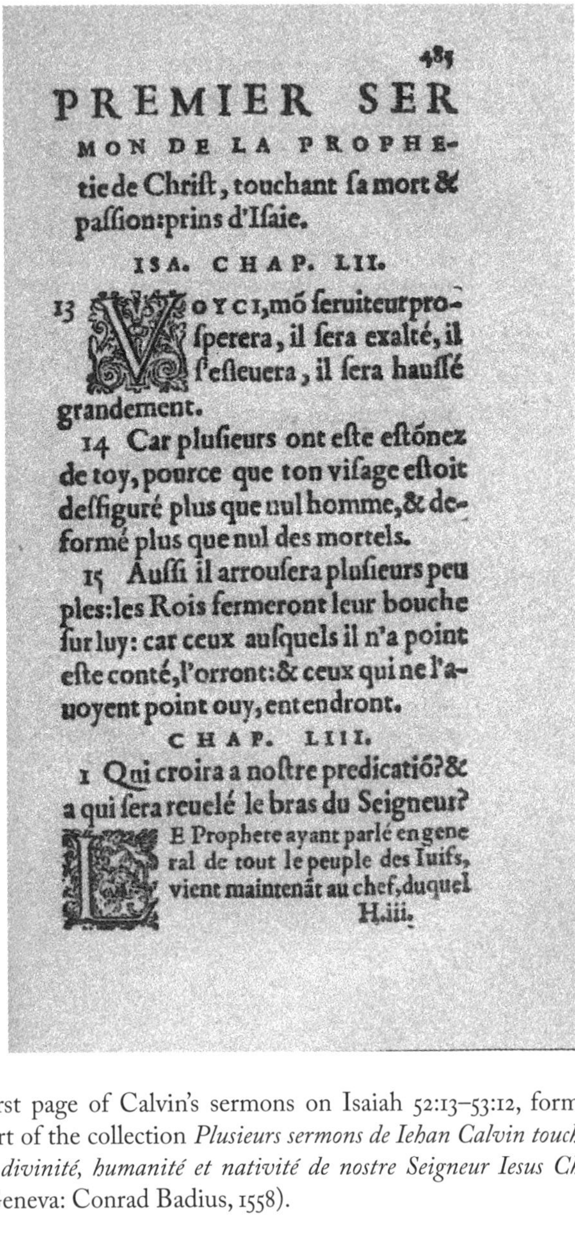

485

PREMIER SER
MON DE LA PROPHE-
tie de Chriſt, touchant ſa mort &
paſſion: prins d'Iſaie.

ISA. CHAP. LII.

13 VOYCI, mõ ſeruiteur pro-
ſperera, il ſera exalté, il
ſ'eſleuera, il ſera hauſſé
grandement.
14 Car pluſieurs ont eſte eſtõnez
de toy, pource que ton viſage eſtoit
deſſiguré plus que nul homme, & de-
formé plus que nul des mortels.
15 Auſſi il arrouſera pluſieurs peu
ples: les Rois fermeront leur bouche
ſur luy: car ceux auſquels il n'a point
eſte conté, l'orront: & ceux qui ne l'a-
uoyent point ouy, entendront.

CHAP. LIII.

1 Qui croira a noſtre predicatiõ? &
a qui ſera reuelé le bras du Seigneur?

LE Prophete ayant parlé en gene
ral de tout le peuple des Iuifs,
vient maintenãt au chef, duquel

H.iii.

First page of Calvin's sermons on Isaiah 52:13–53:12, forming part of the collection *Plusieurs sermons de Iehan Calvin touchant la divinité, humanité et nativité de nostre Seigneur Iesus Christ* (Geneva: Conrad Badius, 1558).

BEHOLD MY SERVANT

SERMONS ON ISAIAH 52:13–53:12

John Calvin

Translated from the French of 1558

by

Robert White

THE BANNER OF TRUTH TRUST

THE BANNER OF TRUTH TRUST

Head Office
3 Murrayfield Road
Edinburgh, EH12 6EL
UK

North America Office
610 Alexander Spring Road
Carlisle, PA 17015
USA

banneroftruth.org

First Banner of Truth edition 2025

ISBN
Print: 978 1 80040 508 0
Epub: 978 1 80040 509 7

*

Typeset in 11/15 pt Adobe Caslon Pro at
The Banner of Truth Trust, Edinburgh

Printed in the USA by
Versa Press, Inc.,
East Peoria, IL

CONTENTS

Behold my servant, whom I uphold,
my chosen, in whom my soul delights.
I have put my Spirit upon him,
he will bring forth justice to the nations.

(Isa. 42:1)

It is too light a thing that you should be my servant,
to raise up the tribes of Jacob
and to restore the preserved of Israel.
I will give you as a light to the nations,
that my salvation may reach to the end of the earth.

(Isa. 49:6)

INTRODUCTION

IT is clear from a reading of the Gospels that the title 'Son of man' was Jesus' preferred self-designation. The title derives from Daniel 7:13-14, where a figure of human appearance comes with the clouds of heaven to the Ancient of Days and receives from him everlasting dominion and a kingdom which cannot be destroyed. On Jesus' lips, however, the significance of the title is radically altered. The Son of man will indeed be raised to glory and to universal kingship (Matt. 25:31-46; 26:64), but only after he has donned the mantle of Isaiah's Suffering Servant, 'despised and rejected by men, a man of sorrows and acquainted with grief' (Isa. 53:3). So powerful is this latter role in Jesus' experience that, for a time, and particularly in the first three Gospels, the heavenly vocation of the Son is entirely submerged by the earthly travails of the Servant. 'How,' Jesus asks his disciples, 'is it written of the Son of man that he should suffer many things and be treated with contempt?' (Mark 9:12). Only in Isaiah is it 'written'; only in Isaiah does suffering lead to exaltation, the cross to the crown.

Isaiah's prophecy of the Servant's undeserved suffering on behalf of the 'many' is an essential point of reference in the Evangelists' account of Jesus' ministry, passion and death. The Servant Songs are cited explicitly in Matthew 8:17 and 12:17, in Luke 22:37 and in John 12:28. They lie close to the surface, however, whenever Jesus is said to contemplate the circumstances and manner of his death (Matt. 16:21; 20:18; Mark 8:31; 10:33-34;

14:21; Luke 17:25), and whenever he teaches the nature of true service (Mark 9:35; 10:42-45; Luke 22:25-27).

The Book of Acts and the witness of the apostles to Christ similarly reflect the influence of the Servant Songs, and notably of the fourth (Isa. 52:13–53:12). To the Jews in Jerusalem Peter boldly proclaims Jesus to be God's servant—God's holy servant—whom God has glorified by raising him from the dead, and through whom forgiveness, healing and life may be had (Acts 3:13-16, 26; 4:27-30). It was Philip's explanation of Isaiah 53:7-8 which, in the world of the diaspora, brought the Ethiopian eunuch to faith. In the Letter to the Romans, Paul's declaration of acquittal secured for many by Christ's obedience inevitably recalls the work of the Servant, by whose knowledge 'many are accounted righteous' (Rom. 5:19; Isa. 53:11). The self-emptying of the incarnate Son which the apostle so movingly describes to his Philippian readers, in essence replicates the pattern set by the Servant: 'exalted and lifted up', he nevertheless submits to death 'as an offering for sin' (Phil. 2:6-8; Isa. 52:13; 53:8, 10). In the same way Peter's exhortation to patient suffering appeals to Christ's example in terms drawn directly from Isaiah's text: 'He committed no sin; no guile was found on his lips. When he was reviled, he did not revile in return … He bore our sins in his body on the tree … By his wounds you have been healed. For you were straying like sheep …' (1 Pet. 2:22-25). In no other Old Testament book are the events of Calvary more startlingly foretold. No Old Testament prophet stands closer to Christ's cross than does Isaiah.

* * *

Beginning in 1546 or 1547, Calvin had spent three years lecturing on Isaiah to his theological students. On the basis of his lectures a commentary had appeared in 1551, dedicated to the young king of England, Edward VI.[1] Five years, however, were to pass before the Reformer undertook to expound Isaiah to his Genevan congregation. His was the last prophetic book to be chosen, since in earlier years Calvin had preached on Jeremiah, on all but two of the minor prophets, on Daniel and on Ezekiel. Following a long sermon series on Deuteronomy, the preacher took up the Book of Isaiah in July 1556—a mammoth task, involving, as was Calvin's custom, a verse-by-verse exposition of the entire book, and made more burdensome by a long period of ill health which forced him to retire temporarily from the pulpit. The series was not completed until late August 1559. In all, 343 sermons on Isaiah were recorded by Calvin's regular stenographer, Denis Raguenier, the resulting transcripts filling six bound volumes, two of which, the first and the last, were subsequently lost.[2]

It is a remarkable fact that, despite the prominent position of Isaiah in the Old Testament canon, and despite the high demand for Calvin's sermons in printed form, only eleven sermons from the Isaiah series were published in the Reformer's lifetime: four on the Song of Hezekiah (Isa. 38), and seven on the fourth of the Servant Songs (Isa. 52:13–53:12). The latter appeared in July 1558, fully a year before the Isaiah series was completed, not as an independent publication but as part of a collection of twenty-six sermons, issued by Genevan printer Conrad Badius under the title *Plusieurs sermons touchant la divinité, humanité et nativité de nostre Seigneur Iesus Christ. Item, touchant sa passion, mort,*

[1] A revised edition was to follow in 1559, dedicated to Elizabeth I. Cf. T. H. L. Parker, *Calvin's Old Testament Commentaries* (Louisville, KY: Westminster/John Knox Press, 1993), pp. 23-25.

[2] The loss has, in part, been made good by the discovery in London, in 1995, of three manuscript volumes containing all of Calvin's sermons on Isa. 24–66. Sermons on Isa. 13–66 are now in print, published in part by Neukirchener Verlag (Neukirchen-Vluyn, 1961, 1995, 2012) = *Supplementa calviniana* II, III, IV1/2; and in part by Droz (Geneva, 2023) = I. Calvini opera omnia, V/13.

resurrection, ascension et dernier advenement.[3] The centrepiece of the collection consists of nine sermons preached in Holy Week of 1557 or 1558, and based on Matthew's narrative of Christ's passion, death and resurrection (Matt. 26–28). To complement these, however, the publisher added seven sermons which Calvin had just finished preaching on Isaiah 52:13–53:12, copies of which were fetched from Raguenier's workshop, we must assume, almost as soon as the ink was dry.[4] It is these sermons which we have translated here from the French of 1558.

* * *

In approaching Isaiah's text, Calvin was well acquainted with the work of earlier exegetes. From time to time the Servant had been identified with Cyrus II, king of Persia, on the basis of passages such as Isaiah 41:25, 44:28–45:1 and 46:11, which cast him in the role of God's instrument and Israel's deliverer.[5] Jewish commentators had envisaged the Servant either as a single individual—a Messianic figure, a scion perhaps of David's house, a prophet whose power lay in his total submission to God's will—or as Israel itself, considered as a corporate personality whose vocation was to suffer, to be revived and to bear witness before the nations to God's truth. Faithful to apostolic and patristic tradition, the Reformer views the Servant as embodying, in all essential details, the life, work and mission of Jesus Christ.

Tradition does not, however, entirely explain Calvin's practice. Theology also has its role to play. It is the eternity of the Son as Redeemer, Mediator and Head of the church which for Calvin

[3] Details in Rodolphe Peter and Jean-François Gilmont, *Bibliotheca calviniana*, 3 vols (Geneva: Droz, 1991-2000), II, pp. 676-81.

[4] As Peter and Gilmont have shown, an interval of only twelve days separates Calvin's last sermon on the Servant's Song from its appearance in print (*Bibliotheca calviniana*, II, p. 680).

[5] See below, Sermon 5 (p. 80), where Calvin attributes this view, which he terms false and corrupt, to Servetus among others.

explains his presence—his omnipresence—in the Old Testament Scriptures. As the Reformer writes in his commentary on the first Servant Song:

> Whenever the prophets promise anything difficult to believe, they are accustomed at once to mention Christ, in whom are confirmed all the promises which would otherwise be doubtful and uncertain. 'In Christ,' says Paul, 'are the Yes and Amen' (2 Cor. 1:2). What dealings could we have with God unless there is a mediator who stands between us? ... Without the gracious work of Christ, we would have no share in salvation or in any other blessing ... To Christ, then, let us come: without him God cannot be propitious to us, unless we know ourselves to be in his body, among the children of God. It will be evident that, from the very beginning, the things that are said can apply to no one else.[6]

So evident is this application to the preacher, and no doubt to his hearers, that it is only when his fourth sermon is almost done that proof of the Servant's identity is furnished by explicit appeal to the story of Philip's encounter with the Ethiopian eunuch: '"Who is the prophet speaking of, himself or someone else?" Then Philip opened his lips, and starting from this Scripture he preached Jesus to him' (Acts 8:35-36).

In expounding the Servant Song, Calvin does no more, in a sense, than move back and forth between the opposing themes of the Servant's heavenly mission and his earthly sufferings. The pattern is set from the very beginning: he who enjoys God's high favour and who excels all others in rank is, in human terms, both in appearance and reputation, an object less of pity than contempt.

The Servant is the Son, coequal with the Father and the Holy Spirit in the unity of the Godhead; he is of the same essence,

[6] Comm. Isa. 42:1 (*CO* 37:57-58).

worthy of the same honour and privy to the same eternal counsel. With the assumption of our nature, he does not cease to be God—one person, two natures—but enters the dimension of time and space over which lies the shadow of the cross. Without abandoning his rights, he sets them aside for a time in pursuit of his mission. He ventures all regardless—*il s'est jeté à l'abandon*, is Calvin's striking phrase—in order to accomplish the work committed to him.[7]

The mission which Isaiah assigns to the Servant has no parallel in the rest of the Old Testament Scriptures. Nevertheless, the prophet's perspective is not in spirit different from that of his contemporaries, Amos and Hosea, or of their successors. As Geerhardus Vos has pointed out, unlike the earlier prophets from Samuel to David, who preached repentance and a return to the purified cult of the past, the writing prophets thought less in terms of reconstruction than of renewal—a new order in which a cleansed people would render God true obedience and lasting worship. 'In this second period,' Vos writes, 'the prophet now knows that not repair but regeneration of the present lies in the womb of the future.'[8] The Servant is thus God's uniquely chosen agent through whom all will be made new.

Throughout his sermons on these key chapters of Isaiah Calvin focuses on two simple but essential questions: What did Christ the Servant come to do? What fruit or benefit accrues to those who trust in his work? The preacher's answers are briefly examined here.

The Servant's work

For all its varied imagery, Isaiah's prophecy describes the Servant's work in unilateral terms: his work is to reverse the

[7] Sermon 7.

[8] Geerhardus Vos, *Biblical Theology: Old and New Testaments* (Grand Rapids, MI: Eerdmans, 1948), p. 207.

consequences of man's sin, by himself bearing the burden of our iniquities and by accepting the punishment which was owed to us, so that, acquitted of our guilt, we might be accounted just and fully reconciled to God. In a word, his work is to make atonement by means of what, in Luther's phrase, is a 'joyful exchange': his innocence for our guilt, his righteousness for our sin. The Servant is both a sin-bearer and a peace-maker.

For Calvin, it is the Old Testament rite of the priestly sin-offering and of intercessory prayer (Lev. 4:1-14) which provides the best insight into the Servant's work. His life ('soul') is made an offering for sin (Isa. 53:10). How necessary that offering was, is made clear by Calvin's description of us, the unredeemed, as 'spiritual lepers, made rotten by our iniquities'.[9] Frequent appeals to the Letter to the Hebrews allow the preacher to establish that the Servant's self-offering is expiatory, placatory and purificatory. By paying the penalty, death, prescribed by the law, the Servant makes full amends: the demands of God's justice are satisfied. Not only so, but by the Servant's vicarious atonement God's wrath against sinners has been put away and his judgment stayed. Propitiation has been made. Finally, from the wounds the Servant bore, from the bruising he suffered, from the blood he shed, come cleansing and purification.

Calvin, however, is no less concerned with the quality of the Servant's work than he is with its result. He characterizes it, in the first place, as a work of pure grace, an unhoped-for display of God's mercy toward the undeserving. 'Jesus Christ was imprisoned …, that we might go free; he was condemned, while we are absolved; he was exposed to every form of shame, while our honour is secure.'[10]

Particular emphasis is laid on the costly nature of the atonement. It is a work of supreme difficulty, involving not only the

[9] Sermon 3.
[10] Sermon 5.

mental and physical agony of innocent suffering, but the experience of spiritual dereliction—for that is how Calvin understands Christ's 'descent into hell'—as the Son is 'made sin for us who knew no sin' (2 Cor. 5:21), so forfeiting the Father's fellowship and undergoing judgment at his hand. That Calvin so often calls Christ's work a 'remedy' for sin implies no simple solution to the problem of our estrangement from God. The remedy is attained at fearful cost to the Physician himself. It is by the Servant's *stripes* that we are healed (Isa. 53:5).

Costly as it is, the Servant's work is nevertheless voluntary, willingly done in obedience to the one who sent him. 'The obedience of our Lord Jesus Christ,' comments Calvin, 'is like a cloak which covers all our transgressions.'[11] Here the Gospel of John guides the preacher's exposition, with its frequent reminders that the Son is not coerced: he delights to do the will of the Father, and freely lays down his life for those whom the Father has given him; he and the Father are one (John 4:34; 10:15, 29-30).

Obedience alone does not account for the Servant's act of self-giving. He yields up his life, and God accepts it as sufficient recompense, out of love for the lost and despairing, and out of pity for those who lie in Satan's bonds. The Son's love, like that of the Father, is limitless. The preacher remarks that in speaking of 'the many' (Isa. 53:11), the prophet really means 'all'. 'Scripture,' he continues, 'is not speaking of three or four when it says that God so loved the world … (John 3:16). Our Lord Jesus suffered for all, and there is no excuse for any, great or small, since it is in him that we have salvation.'[12]

How we may benefit

Incomparable as the Servant's work is, it would count for little if it were not also, at the same time, effective—if, that is, it failed to

[11] Sermon 5.
[12] Sermon 7.

benefit those on whose behalf it was accomplished. What fruit, then, may be derived from it, and how may it be appropriated?

Passing from doctrine to application, the preacher affirms that those who would gain from the Servant's atoning work must 'come to Jesus Christ'. So often does the phrase occur in these seven sermons that it must be regarded as Calvin's standard mode of appeal. Its apparent simplicity, however, needs to be rounded out if justice is to be done to the preacher's thought and intention. Mere acceptance of the fact that atonement has been made is not enough to evoke a response or to authenticate the value of the Servant's person and work. From Christ's first appearance among men, from the moment of the incarnation, we are confronted with a mystery so complete as to be unfathomable. That the infinite should become finite, the immortal, mortal, and the all-gracious, the all-despised, defies both language and imagination.

To come to Jesus Christ, therefore, begins with the honest recognition of our ignorance—of our culpable ignorance which, without grace, leads us inevitably to regard the cross as foolish and, worse, as offensive. To come to him is to accept the scandal of the cross and to renounce our cherished wisdom and autonomy. Humility, the abandonment of pride, is inseparable from conversion. So also is gratitude, thankfulness for the grace revealed in the gospel—an abiding sense of our indebtedness to God's mercy and goodness, which overlook not merely our lack of merit but our ingrained hostility, our native rebelliousness. And since gratitude involves the acknowledgment of God's goodwill toward us, what other response is possible but trust—trust which, enabled by the Spirit, makes us one with Christ and members of God's family? 'He who is the beloved,' says Calvin, 'must accept us, and so unite himself to us that we might have by adoption what is his by nature.'[13]

[13] Sermon 5.

No one who comes to Jesus Christ will be disappointed. Calvin is at pains to encourage his congregation to accept the offer of salvation made to them, by insisting on the all-sufficiency of Christ. From Christ our fountainhead, he says, we may draw everything that we lack. 'He has sufficient to satisfy all of us. We should not fear that the fullness of grace which he possesses will ever run dry. He will give his part and portion to each one who comes seeking it in him.'[14] It could hardly be otherwise, since in Jesus Christ we find not only a Redeemer, but a faithful Mediator, an Advocate who pleads our case, an Intercessor who prays for us. 'Our Lord Jesus Christ speaks on our behalf, and our prayers and supplications are sanctified by him.'[15]

There remains one last problem for the preacher to confront: the problem of unbelief. If Christ's redeeming work is so manifestly to our advantage, so generous in its scope and so incalculable in its consequences, why are we so reluctant to accept it, so slow to enjoy its fruits? Why are humility, gratitude and faith so often absent when the gospel is proclaimed?

The preacher does not need to press his text hard in order to find an answer. It is found in the opening verse of Isaiah 53: 'Who has believed our report?' Only God, explains Calvin, can cause the blind to see. Through his Holy Spirit, without whose gracious work none can come to Christ, 'God is secretly active in his elect, so that they feel as it were his arm and his power.' 'The gospel,' he continues, 'is hidden from the reprobate; it is a privilege given to few people, to those he has elected and adopted in order to bring them to eternal life.'[16] Election, like the incarnation itself, is a mystery, hidden in God's eternal counsel. It is not for us to probe that mystery, but to respond of our own accord, and in all conscience, to the gospel of grace. Election, in

[14] Sermon 3.
[15] Sermon 7.
[16] Sermon 2.

Calvin's preaching, explains unbelief; it does not compel, still less justify it.

* * *

It was Calvin's habit to reserve his Sunday sermons for exposition of a New Testament text or, occasionally, a Psalm. He preached on weekdays in alternate weeks on an Old Testament book. Existing records allow us to date his seven sermons on Isaiah 52:13–53 precisely: the first was delivered on Saturday, 18 June, and the remainder between Monday, 27 June and Saturday, 2 July 1558. They were, as we have seen, swiftly typeset, printed and within a few days released for sale as part of an attractive sermon miscellany.

Calvin's sermons enjoyed a strong following in Elizabethan England. The contents of the Badius edition of 1558 were translated into English by Thomas Stocker in 1581 and were issued under the title *Divers sermons concerning the Divinitie, Humanitie and Nativitie of our Lorde Iesus Christe*. Almost four centuries later two further English versions appeared, produced independently of each other: *The Gospel according to Isaiah: Seven Sermons on Isaiah 53*, translated by Leroy Nixon (Grand Rapids, Michigan: Wm. B. Eerdmans, 1953); *Sermons on Isaiah's Prophecy of the Death and Passion of Christ*, translated by T. H. L. Parker (London: James Clarke, 1956). Of the two, Parker's is better in terms both of accuracy and style. Seventy years, however, have now passed since these works first saw the light of day. It is therefore hoped that a new generation of readers will welcome what is offered here—a fresh translation of Calvin's exposition of what is effectively the clearest Old Testament articulation of the Christian gospel.

Our translation is based on the text established by the nineteenth-century editors of the Reformer's collected works,

Calvini opera quae supersunt omnia.[17] Careful comparison has, however, been made with the original Badius edition of 1558. Modern conventions regarding punctuation, sentence length and paragraph divisions have been observed. Sermon headings are my own. Scripture citations are translated as they stand: Calvin often cites from memory and frequently paraphrases the biblical text. Biblical references which the *CO* editors reproduce from the original text have been corrected where necessary, and additional references have been added. I have included the extempore prayer with which each sermon ends, together with the prayer for illumination and the intercessory prayer which Calvin used in his weekday services. A small number of explanatory notes has been supplied.

I wish, finally, to thank the members of The Banner of Truth Trust for their willingness to publish, and the Trust's staff for their generous help and advice.

ROBERT WHITE
6 January 2025
Sydney

[17] Ed. G. Baum, E. Cunitz and E. Reuss, 59 vols., Brunswick and Berlin: C. A. Schwetschke & Son, 1863–1900. (Hereafter cited as *CO*.) The sermons on Isa. 52:12–53 will be found in *CO* 35:595-688. The most recent edition of the text is that prepared by Max Engammare: *Sermons sur le livre d'Esaïe* (52–59), Neukirchen-Vluyn: Neukirchener Verlag, 2012 = *Supplementa calviniana* IV/1, pp. 42-150.

I

THE SERVANT OF THE LORD

Behold, my servant will prosper; he will be exalted, he will be lifted up, he will rise very high. [14] *For many were appalled by you, because your face was more marred than any man's, and disfigured more than that of any mortal.* [15] *Therefore he will sprinkle many peoples. Kings will shut their mouths at him; those who had not been told will hear him, and those who had not heard him will understand.*

[1] *Who will believe what we preach? And to whom will the arm of the Lord be revealed?* (Isa. 52:13–53:1).

THE prophet, having spoken in general terms about all the Jewish people, now comes to his main point, on which everything which he has previously said depends. The Jews' redemption had our Lord Jesus Christ as its sole foundation, since it is in him that all of God's promises are fulfilled (2 Cor. 1:20). For a long time now the Redeemer had been promised, but with the apparent extinction of David's line, the hopes of God's faithful people were very likely ended. It had been said that God would forever establish a king whom he would set on David's throne, and that as long as sun and moon were in the sky, that kingdom would be maintained and preserved (2 Sam. 7:12-13, 16; 1 Chron. 17:11-14; Psa. 89:35-37). And even if the whole world were to perish, the kingdom would be so strong and firm that all would see that it was fully consecrated to God.

Nevertheless, at that very point, the kingdom begins to shrink, and soon afterwards, little by little, it goes into decline, until the second last king is taken away captive; all the royal family is deported, and the line is more or less cut off (2 Kings 24:15; 2 Chron. 36:10). The last king was put in place on the whim of an unbeliever, an enemy of all religion,[1] but having rebelled against him, he is captured and his eyes put out; he is brought to trial, his children are killed and, reviled by all, he is condemned. The temple and every house is burned (2 Kings 25:6-7, 9; Jer. 52:9-11). What might we make of that?[2]

It was necessary, therefore, for the prophet to assure the Jews that ultimately God would have compassion on them and would bring them back from their captivity. He most certainly needed to show them that what had formerly been said to Abraham had not been said in vain—namely, that in his seed all the nations on earth would be blessed (Gen. 12:3). There would be a king enthroned from David's line, whose dominion would have no end; it would be everlasting. That is why Isaiah now concentrates his attention on our Lord Jesus Christ, in order that men should be absolutely certain of what he had said earlier about the people's redemption and return.

We noted previously that our Lord Jesus Christ was called *the Servant of the Lord* (Isa. 42:1), since he yielded full obedience for the sake of our salvation. Of course, he was the Lord of glory

[1] Nebuchadnezzar. Cf. 2 Kings 24:17-20.

[2] Judah first sought to throw off the Babylonian yoke in the reign of Jehoiakim (2 Kings 24:1); the conflict ended in defeat in 597 BC, in the reign of Jehoiachin, his successor. A further insurrection involving Zedekiah, the last king of Judah, led to a long siege of Jerusalem and to the disaster of 587 which the preacher goes on to describe.—Despite his Christocentric reading of Isaiah's text, and within the limits allowed by the sermon *genre*, Calvin is too careful an interpreter to ignore the historical context in which the prophecy is set. Cf. David L. Puckett, *John Calvin's Exegesis of the Old Testament* (Louisville, KY: Westminster John Knox Press, 1995), pp. 67-72.

and the Head of the angels, before whom every knee must bow. So when the title 'Servant' is applied to him, remember that it was because he took our nature upon himself, and that it was in this nature that he chose not only to humble himself but to make himself as nothing (Phil. 2:7-8). By his obedience he had to repair our transgressions and iniquity: as he said to John the Baptist, it was necessary for him to fulfil all righteousness (Matt. 3:15). That, then, is how, although all majesty belongs to him, and although he is everlasting God, our Lord Jesus Christ chose a lowlier rank, for he was clothed with our flesh and became one like us.

There is no inconsistency here. Although there was no change in respect of his divine nature, he had to humble himself, since we regard him as the Mediator between God and ourselves. In the same way he is said to have been born under the law (Gal. 4:4), even though he was no man's debtor and was the one appointed to rule us; to him we must render all obedience. Even so he chose that particular rank so as to deliver us from the yoke we could not bear, for the law would have been a burden which would have crushed us all, if our Lord Jesus Christ had not, by bearing it, set us free. We should not think it strange, then, if he is called God's Servant, since he did not shrink from becoming, at the same time, our servant, which is an even greater thing.

If we reflect on our condition, it is mere futility. We are miserable earthworms, controlled by the devil and by sin. Nevertheless we see the Son of God stooping so low as to make himself our servant. As Paul says, he is a minister of the circumcision (Rom. 15:8). Furthermore, the prophet used this term in order to teach us that everything said here about him is for the common good and salvation of the whole church. Consider, then, the task to which Jesus Christ was called: he was to be the Redeemer of all who believe, of all God's elect. Accordingly, since this mission has been entrusted to him, since this is his calling, let us not doubt that what we are taught here about him is common to all of us and is to our advantage, as will be clear from what comes later. Such is the prophet's meaning here.

Isaiah therefore says that Jesus Christ, having been called to the task of saving all who are his, *will prosper; he will be raised on high and will be wonderfully exalted.* This was meant to arm the faithful against the trials which they might meet before Jesus Christ appeared in majesty—before, that is, he who is everlasting God and full of glory was made manifest in the flesh. For, as we have already said, when the Jews were taken away to Babylon, all that was noble in David's line was lost; everything had been swept away. True, when some of the people returned, Zerubbabel was regarded as their governor and leader; but there was no royal crown, only a man of honourable reputation, for the people still had a certain respect for the house of David (Ezra 2:2; Hag. 1:1).[3] So, as I say, Zerubbabel was obeyed, but there was nothing resembling real kingship. The faithful thus had to be equipped to meet trial and tribulation. God had to assure them that the Redeemer would appear, and that even if the earth had to open and bring him forth from its very depths in order to raise him on high, this must of necessity happen.

Here, then, beyond any doubt, the prophet is contrasting two quite contrary things. He first suggests that Jesus Christ would long remain concealed, sunk, as it were, in some bottomless chasm. And even when he did come forth, there would be no great display which would earn him men's esteem. On the contrary, he would be rejected, held in such contempt that no one would think that he could bring his people to salvation. The prophet expresses this more clearly when he says, *he was more marred than any man, and no comeliness was seen in him.* It is as if he was not worthy to be ranked among God's creatures, but deserved to be looked upon with loathing, his very appearance

[3] Zerubbabel was the grandson of Jehoiachin and was thus of royal descent.

inspiring horror. This is what the prophet has in mind when he says that Jesus Christ was lifted high.

Now at first glance these two things appear contradictory. We might think it inconsistent that on the one hand men should look for Jesus Christ yet fail to recognize or find him; and on the other that when they do see him, they reject him! They find nothing in him worth admiring, yet God lifts him up, exalts him and so raises him on high that he surpasses every notion we might have of his majesty in this world. We might think that these two things cannot be reconciled, any more than fire can mix with water. Nevertheless, Isaiah declares that we must hope that God will do his work, and that small beginnings will not prevent his purpose from attaining its full goal. That is why he says that God's Servant will be raised up, wonderfully exalted and lifted high. This was indeed a difficult test to master. Nor is it enough that God should tell us in one word what he proposed to do. When we understand all that stood in his way and made his words appear impossible, we should be strong in faith, recognizing that we have what we need to overcome the obstacles that lie ahead—the things, that is, which stop us trusting in God's promises.

It is as if the prophet were saying, 'Friends, wait for the Lord to raise up the Redeemer, for he will do it.' And if we object, 'Yes, but how? This is a strange way to go about it!' 'Cease doubting: in God there is a power which is hidden from you. If you are still in doubt, if you are still in two minds, if you are still inclined to argue, if my sole word is not enough for you, resist these thoughts. Steady yourselves, defy your unbelief and decide that, come what may, God will do more than you think, imagine or expect.' That is what Isaiah means by these three or four words. They all point to the same idea.

'His face,' says the prophet, 'was marred. There was no form or comeliness in him.' He was cut off, as it were, from all human companionship. He was not worthy to take his place among mortal creatures. A fuller explanation will follow in due course, but already Isaiah makes it clear that, as they waited for their Redeemer, the Jews must close their eyes to all the things we normally look for. They were instead to make way for faith and to trust assuredly in God's goodness, however much reality belied their expectation.

This was true not only of the Lord Jesus Christ himself, but of the entire course of his gospel and of the whole process by which he upholds and rules his faithful people. If, then, we want to be assured of our salvation in Jesus Christ, we must first of all not be ashamed that he was thus marred in the eyes of men, and that, having been sent into the world, he was considered abhorrent and accursed. Later too his gospel became an object of infamy and shame, as is also the case today (1 Cor. 1:21-25). And if we are ashamed to receive Jesus Christ as our crucified Lord, we are most certainly excluded from all hope of salvation. How, after all, can we be saved by him? How can the inheritance of heaven be ours, unless he was made a curse for us, not only in the eyes of men but by the very mouth of God his Father? (Gal. 3:13). In this way Jesus Christ, who is the fount of every blessing, bore our sins. He became like the sacrifices of old which were called sin-offerings, since it was necessary for God's wrath to be revealed in them, and that, through them, we might be pardoned and set free. Again, how is Jesus Christ our life, if not because by dying he swallowed up death? And how does he raise us up, except by entering into the depths of hell, that is, by bearing the terrors which beset us because of sin, and which would have overwhelmed us?

God had always to be our judge. That he should be our enemy is the most frightful thing there is. Thus Jesus Christ had to come in as our surety, as the one who was to pay on our behalf and to bear our condemnation, so that we might be forgiven. We should not think it strange, then, if we see that he was marred. To our way of thinking such a thing is foolish. Let us acknowledge, as Paul himself writes, that the foolishness of God surpasses all the wisdom of the world (1 Cor. 1:25). What he calls God's foolishness is our Lord's utter humiliation, for if we judged by this fact alone, we would surely say it was absurd. What? He who was to be worshipped in heaven and on earth should be exposed to such abuse? And for what reason? This is how, in their pride and arrogance, men will always with unparalleled rashness and audacity condemn all that God has done for their redemption. Nevertheless, God in his counsel will prove that he is wiser than we could ever conceive.

So we take it as absolutely certain that if our Lord Jesus Christ was held in contempt, not only humbling himself but, in Paul's words, becoming as nothing (Phil. 2:7), we should not fail to ascribe to him the honour he deserves. His glory was in no way diminished on that account, even though not everyone acknowledged it. All the more lustre was added to his goodness. We ought to thrill with awe when we see that God's Son, he who was the express image of God his Father (Heb. 1:3), did not shrink from appearing as one marred, all in order to restore God's image in us. For there is no question that we are spotted and stained, and that if we are to appear before God we will be cast out, unless Jesus Christ has placed his mark on us, by means of which we can come to God and find favour and acceptance with him. When, therefore, we read that he appeared as a man marred, we should look to ourselves, knowing that it was necessary for him to assume all our spots and stains, so that we might be purged and cleansed of them and might now bring to God's judgment seat righteousness and holiness. These would not be ours if God did not impart them to us in Jesus Christ.

That said, the prophet adds: *Kings themselves will shut their mouths at him when he is exalted thus*—when, that is, they behold him changed in a way they could never have imagined. Here Isaiah teaches us not to be thoughtless in our judgment when we see our Lord Jesus Christ abased and made indeed as nothing. We must consider the end in view, that to which God the Father has led him. The fact is that a name has been given him which is above every name, and that every knee will bow before him, as Paul says in the second chapter of Philippians (Phil. 2:9-10). For when the apostle exhorts us to be self-controlled and not to have a high opinion of ourselves, he sets our Lord Jesus Christ before us as a model and a mirror. 'He who is true God,' he writes, 'and who would not have thought it robbery to appear in heavenly glory, made himself as nothing, and took upon himself the status and condition of a servant.' He went willingly to the cross and did not refuse a death so shameful and accursed in the sight of God and man. All this he did in order to take upon himself what we ourselves deserved. 'Therefore,' says Paul, 'the Father has exalted him and given him a name such that all creatures, high and low, should pay him homage, and all confess that he is truly in the glory of God his Father' (Phil. 2:9-11).

If, then, we wish to behold what God's majesty is like and to glorify him as he deserves, we must come to our Lord Jesus Christ. This, in essence, is the prophet's meaning here. The fact that Jesus Christ was humbled for a time should not close the door to our believing in him, and to our placing our trust in him. We must keep in view the final goal, so that when we speak of his death, we should pass immediately to his resurrection, combining the two into one. That Jesus Christ chose to suffer in the weakness which he inherited from us, and that he rose again in the power of his Holy Spirit, are two inseparable things. And in rising he showed himself to be the true Son of God, as Paul declares in both 1 Timothy and 2 Corinthians, and also in the first chapter of Romans (1 Tim. 3:16; 2 Cor. 13:4; Rom. 1:4). That is what Isaiah is driving at in this passage.

We said before that all of this is true not only of Jesus Christ but also of his gospel. When the gospel was preached, how was he acknowledged, and how obeyed? We see that those to whom he gave authority were not only mocked and condemned by men, but were beaten, scourged and finally consigned to a shameful death. We need, then, to overcome all such obstacles to faith and, arming ourselves with the prophet's words, let us look to the goal which our Lord Jesus Christ attained. Let us shut our mouths to show how much we are in awe; let us cease protesting the way the faithless do when they twitter on. On they go, never managing to come to our Lord Jesus Christ and to do him homage. They have their reasons, they believe, for arguing against him.

We, on the other hand, when we consider all that our Lord finally achieved—the purpose and fruit of the death and passion he suffered for our salvation—our mouths will indeed be shut. Scripture, when it speaks this way, points to a calm and sensible consideration of God's works. As long as our mouths are open, we insist on entering the debate and making a reasoned case; we abandon God and turn our backs on all that he has done. When, however, Scripture says that every mouth should be shut and that we should be silent before God (Hab. 2:20; Rom. 3:19), it seeks to teach us that we should keep our feelings captive and our tongues bridled, quietly confessing that God is worthy to be glorified in the person of his only Son.

Now if this is said of kings, what is the case with ordinary folk? Remember the sequence which Isaiah follows here. First, he shows how our Lord Jesus had to become as a man marred, as one whom the world rejected. Then by the Holy Spirit we are warned not to think this strange or to fail to embrace him with true faith. And although the cross, a gallows abhorrent to men, might deter us and completely alienate us from him, we are nevertheless to make him—Jesus Christ crucified—all our boast. Moreover we must not dwell only on the fact of his suffering, seeing him as a figure of shame—shame willingly undergone on our behalf. No, we are to combine both death and resurrection, knowing that he who was crucified is seated as the deputy of God his Father, exercising sovereign rule and having all authority in heaven and on earth.

This is why, as Isaiah says, he will be exalted. True, although to be raised on a gallows was disgraceful in men's eyes, our Lord mocks the devil by declaring that he will indeed be exalted (John 3:14; 8:28), and that having been so shamed that men will put out their tongues at him and spew forth their evil blasphemies, he will nevertheless take his seat, according to the verse cited earlier from Paul (Col. 2:14-15). The cross was a gallows full of shame; yet it was, in a sense, a triumphal car. Not only did Jesus Christ vanquish the devil; he also taught us that we can now glory in the fact that we are free of all condemnation. Sin has no more power over us (Rom. 6:14). All the devils in hell have been stripped of every claim they had against us. This is how, by faith, we are to ascend to the glory of our Lord Jesus Christ. We need not be ashamed to seek our salvation in his cross, our blessing in his curse, our life in his death, our boasting in the shame he bore, and our joy in his anguish so profound that he sweated blood and water (Luke 22:44). These, in sum, are the things to remember about this passage.

The prophet next declares that *he will sprinkle many nations.* It is true that the word he uses has the figurative sense of 'to speak'. All things considered, however, the natural meaning intended by the prophet is 'sprinkle'. In other words, although Jesus Christ is as a dry and barren block of wood, by his power he will sprinkle the whole world. God will, in one word, work in a way that passes comprehension. The Jews will not have to look to man-made means; they should instead hope that God will surpass anything the world might conceive.

Our minds inevitably reel when people speak to us of miracles or of mysteries—that is, of secrets. We are forced to acknowledge that we are not judges or arbiters competent enough to say: 'This is how it is!' We must worship those things which cannot enter our heads and whose reason is unknown to us. That is something else to bear in mind.

Here, then, is an admonition which is relevant to us. We must allow ourselves to be sprinkled by our Lord Jesus Christ, and although he was only barren in appearance, for nothing worthy of esteem was found in him, when he comes before us and seeks to draw near, let us not rebuff him in our unbelief; let us allow him to enter in through faith.

The prophet goes further, however, declaring that everyone will be sprinkled by our Lord Jesus Christ—that is, by the preaching of the gospel. *'For,'* he says, *'those who have not been told will hear, and those who have not heard will understand.'* Isaiah expands therefore on his theme, explaining that our Lord Jesus Christ was sent by God his Father not only for the Jews (although he had been specifically promised to them), but in order to be the Saviour of the whole world. That this is what Isaiah means is made clear by Paul in the fifteenth chapter of Romans. He applies these very words to his work of mission in foreign lands. There, hastening from place to place, he filled with the gospel every region where no one had ever spoken of God (Rom. 15:20-21). Paul preached not only among the Jews but also among the Gentiles.

The prophet's intention is thus clear. This verse should be for us a key, as it were, which opens the kingdom of heaven to us. If Jesus Christ had been promised only to Abraham's descendants, what good would that have done us? And even if he was their Saviour and Redeemer, it would have been of no use to us: we would have had no part or share in him. Because, however, it had been foretold long before he was sent that he would sprinkle all nations, so that those who had not heard earlier should understand, and those who had not been told would hear—because of that, now that Jesus Christ has come into the world and has done all that is necessary for our salvation, know indeed that our Lord has adopted us. So the message of the gospel is in a way like rain, which gives us a heaven-sent vitality, whereas in fact we are totally barren. And because we are famished and empty of God's grace, we must be fed by the teaching of the gospel, so that, recognizing the merit of the death suffered by our Redeemer and the benefit it brings us, we may find fullness of joy in his life.

It is obvious that Isaiah is not referring here to the Jews, who from infancy were nurtured in the law and accustomed to it. The prophet is reaching out to foreign nations which previously knew nothing but superstition and idolatry. The whole world rejected Israel's God; it despised him, and the Gentiles poured scorn on true religion. Nevertheless, Scripture says that they will hear, and that, having heard, they will understand. With these words the prophet clearly shows from where faith comes: it comes from the hearing of God's word (Rom. 10:17). Yet at the same time he demonstrates that it is not enough for the preaching of the gospel to be drummed into our ears, if it is not also accompanied by understanding. Understanding, however, is not given to everyone: hence what is said here must be confined to God's elect, to those who are renewed by the Holy Spirit.

This is the point which Isaiah expressly makes in the next verse: *Who will believe our message? And to whom will the arm of the Lord be revealed—or displayed?* Here, in the middle of his declaration, the prophet pauses, and cries out as if awe-struck and in wonderment. This is a verse which deserves our close attention. The prophet, as we have seen, urges believers to be courageous and steadfast, as if to say, 'Do not be surprised if there is no mark of nobility in your Redeemer, nothing which is estimable in men's eyes, so that each man spits in his face, derides and even curses him. Do not, however, turn from him in scorn, for God ordained that it should be so. You know how it will end. Our Lord will be taken out of death's abyss and raised on high, there to have authority over every creature. See that you worship the Redeemer who, for your good, humbled himself.' Indeed, as we saw, the prophet compares Jesus Christ to the rain, declaring that God will sprinkle those who have never heard the truth and who have lived like poor brute beasts. 'These people,' he says, 'will be taught, and will be made to share in the salvation won for us. The church of God will spread throughout the world, and those who once blasphemed against God's pure truth will shut their mouths, unless it be to confess soberly and with reverence that there is no God but the God of Israel. He must be honoured, and we must receive and pay homage to his only Son, who is the very image of his glory and majesty (Col. 1:15). Even kings, blinded as they are by arrogance, will be forced to humble themselves and to yield full obedience to him.'

These are Isaiah's marvellous words. Nevertheless, he foresees that when the gospel is preached throughout the world, some will mock, and others will rail furiously against it. Some will not find it to their taste, some will remain obtuse, and some who are hypocrites will lie to God: they will appear to obey the message, but it will only be a sham. Hence the prophet, knowing what evil there is in the world, and foreseeing that men will not listen to God or receive his word with the reverence it deserves, exclaims: 'Who will believe what we teach?' In effect, he is saying this: 'Alas, I preach salvation to the world, but all is lost and hopeless unless, by way of remedy, God sends his only Son to fight against death and the devil, and thus obtains for us righteousness and life.'

This is a message which is meant to sprinkle the whole world; without it we are barren, altogether dry and destitute. Even so

God does not wait for us to ask him to sprinkle us. He anticipates us, generously offering us himself, and with his message he sets before us his only Son. Here he shows himself a Redeemer so worthy of our love that we should accept him unreservedly. Should we not all burn with zeal so that, despising everything else, we embrace the Redeemer now that he has come? Yet so far is this from happening that scarcely one tenth of those who hear are moved in earnest. As experience shows, there are those who jeer, for they despise God and have no more faith or religion than dogs. Everything they are told about the heavenly life they dismiss as fiction. And there are others who are not content simply to scorn God's word. They go much further and are aflame with rage against it. Others again shout their blasphemies out loud, or else want to cling to the ideas which they have hatched in their heads. Then too we see many mindless folk who remain unmoved, displaying no more feeling than stones. Still others make a fine show of godliness, but they are liars and perjurers, no more than frauds and hypocrites.[4]

Such are the things we see, and even if the prophet had not spoken thus, let us open our eyes and see his words fulfilled. Is this not truly frightful, a monstrous sin against nature? Without a doubt it is! Now it could be a serious stumbling block for us when we consider how the world reacts; it could be a barrier preventing us from coming to the gospel. 'What's this?' we might say. 'God's word should be men's sovereign good and happiness. Why then do they reject it? And how can God allow people to mock and resist him, so that he cannot gain a hearing

[4] That the preaching of the gospel meets with very mixed results accords precisely with Calvin's doctrine of election. The fact remains that, as a tireless preacher and pastor, the Reformer grieved to see so many who, in Geneva as elsewhere, refused the offer of salvation or who let it pass them by. As Herman Bavinck aptly remarks, 'It is incorrect to represent the wretched state of the lost as the goal of predestination … The fall, sin and eternal punishment are willed by God, but only in a certain sense and not in the same manner as grace and blessedness.' (*Reformed Dogmatics*, ed. John Bolt, tr. John Vriend, 4 vols, Grand Rapids, MI: Baker Academic, 2003-08, II, p. 299.)

or be given the credit he deserves?' This is how we are tempted not to believe the gospel, as if men's faithlessness detracted from God's truth and diminished the honour which is rightly his!

The prophet, then, has a very good reason for interpolating this verse. If he had simply said the things we noted before—that the Lord Jesus Christ would sprinkle the whole world, that the gospel message would spread everywhere, and that kings would submit to him—we would now be saying: 'Isaiah's words are not meant for our time: it's the exact opposite that we see. Instead of the earth being sprinkled so that salvation is attained, we witness a flood of iniquity! People in their stupidity are hell-bent on rebelling against anything to do with God. The gospel is so little welcome that it is dreadful to behold. So what the prophet foretells can't yet be true.'

This, as I say, might well overturn our faith, if Isaiah had not added this verse to what we noticed earlier. God, we said, sends us his rain in order to give us life; but he does not grant the particular grace of his Holy Spirit to all so that they accept his word. The majority, the unbelieving, will find that their ears are stopped, or else they will be hardened and will be goaded all the more to do evil. There will be others who take no account of the priceless gift imparted to them. So when the prophet speaks of all these things, and when we in fact see them, we should not be alarmed. Instead, let our faith be all the stronger. That, in short, is the lesson for us here.

We should reckon on the fact that the world will never turn to God so that the majority will no longer belong to Satan. They will persist in their mindlessness, preferring to perish rather than accept the gift God offers. People, as we said, differ according to type. Some are mindless; others mock God out of pride, or in their arrogance foolishly condemn all that the gospel contains. Some are immersed in the cares of this world: they are obsessed with their sly and tricky ways and have no taste for anything to do with heaven. Others are so bemused that there is no way of getting any teaching into their heads. When, therefore, we see such things, let us make up our minds that although the gospel is preached, and although God's voice echoes and re-echoes on every hand, many people remain as they have always been. They will not change: for them, all teaching is lifeless and dead.

That is one point. We see, then, that the number of believers is small. Yet we should not fall away, but rather acknowledge that God fulfils the words his mouth has uttered. We are constantly encouraged, then, to gather under his wings, because the world today is full of evil and rebelliousness. We should of course be fearful and more anxious in our walk. If everyone were ready and willing to serve God, there would be plenty of examples all around which would rouse us to labour boldly on. But when it is said that most of those to whom the gospel is preached are like devils, and that evils are seen on every hand so that the world appears to have conspired to alienate us totally from God, we have good cause to walk in fear. For how would it be if God did not miraculously preserve us? Anyone willing to hold to the gospel must therefore be prepared to withstand everything which might make him stumble. And although we may see others who fail to do their duty, we should not turn aside. Supposing we saw the whole world trampling God's word underfoot, we ought to remain loyal to it; and not only so, we should strive all the harder to be obedient to our God, however much the faults and bad examples which we see might turn us away from him. Let us remain honest and upright, for to this God calls us.

That is what we need to remember when we hear the prophet's cry: 'Who will believe what we have heard?' Isaiah assumes that those who believe will be few and far between, and that though the gospel is everywhere proclaimed, if we consider the benefits it has brought, we will find very few who have a living root, who have been restored and remade, whose lives have been changed and who have denied themselves in order to yield wholly to God. We will see, I say, only a small number of people like that.

At the same time the prophet mentions the reason for this, but that is something we cannot explain just now. Faith, we should note, is a particular gift of God. To be familiar with the gospel message, and to have it drummed into our ears, is not all there is. God must touch us and work in us by his secret power, so that we are drawn to him and built up by the preaching which we hear. This point cannot, however, be dealt with for the moment; we will keep it for another day.

Now let us cast ourselves down before the majesty of our good God, acknowledging our faults and praying that he may make us feel them more and more. May we be drawn to him with such repentance that we strive continually throughout our lives to put an end to our defilements, failings and evil desires. May we be delivered from them by the grace of the Holy Spirit, and may we seek only to glorify our God. And since he wills that all praise be given to him in and through his only Son, may we with true humility embrace the Redeemer who is offered to us. And may we all the while be inwardly mortified, so that, being raised to the majesty which has been given to him, we may share in the life he has obtained for us.

2

A ROCK OF OFFENCE

Who will believe what we preach? And to whom will the arm of the Lord be revealed? [2] *He will grow up before him like a young shoot, and like a root in dry ground. He has neither form nor comeliness, and we saw that there was no excellence in him that we might desire him.* [3] *He was despised and rejected among men, a man of sorrows, familiar with infirmity, so that men in their scorn will hide their faces from him, and none will esteem him.* [4] *Truly he bore our weaknesses and carried our sorrows, yet we esteemed him stricken by God, and afflicted* (Isa. 53:1-4).

WE began by pointing out that although the gospel was to be preached throughout the world, it would not be well received by most people. The prophet made this point clear, so that God's children should not be alarmed when they saw the unbelief of those into whose ears the message of salvation had been drummed, and who nevertheless were unwilling to accept it. It is strange indeed that God should call men to him and should try to win them in the kindest and most gracious way possible, but that they should turn away from him and deliberately refuse to come to the salvation which is set before them. It seems impossible, yet this is what experience shows us. As a result, the prophet proclaims that when God with trumpet sound seeks to make his gospel known, it is only a small number who believe.

Isaiah now explains the reason: *God is revealing his power*, with the aim of giving faith to those who, left to their natural understanding, would remain in unbelief. Why is it that we see so many who reject the gospel? Why are so many weary of it, or so offended that they would rather be like those who despise God than draw near to him? Why is this, I ask, if not because we imagine that faith lies in the power of each of us? Isaiah, on the contrary, declares that although God commands that his word be proclaimed to all—that is, to both good and bad—nevertheless he is secretly active in his elect, causing them as it were to feel his arm and power.[1]

Observe, then, that when the gospel is preached it will be like a meaningless sound until our Lord reveals that he is the one speaking. He does not grant this gift to everyone. So God's power is hidden from the reprobate; it is a privilege given to few people, to those he has elected and adopted in order to bring them to eternal life—to those who have his assurance that the gospel is the message of salvation, and that it is the sure truth to which they must hold. That, in brief, is what the prophet Isaiah seeks to convey in this verse.

For our part we must be armed and equipped to meet the obstacle which the devil sets before us. For when we see so many people resisting the gospel—yes, the very greatest, and those highly regarded by men—we are almost led to think that this cannot be God's word. Why do we think that? Our faith is shaken because we depend too much on men. Let us overcome, then, everything which is of the world, and let us recognize that when God speaks, we must submit to him. Even if no one keeps us company, even if everyone is our enemy, let us nevertheless

[1] See the preceding sermon, p. 14, note 4.

receive with purity of faith whatever God declares. And to avoid being overly surprised that people should be so wilful as to war against their God, against the one who created them and who shows himself to them as their Redeemer, understand that this is not given to all, and that faith is a particular gift which God keeps as a treasure for those he has chosen.

Although we know that our duty is to cleave to God, we should realize that faith is not something which of our own accord we give to ourselves: God enlightens us and by his Holy Spirit gives us eyes to see. In doing so he reveals to us his power; that is, he produces so lively an impression in our hearts that we know that the gospel comes not from men, but from him. That, in sum, is what we have to remember about this text. So we should boldly defy the unbelief and obstinacy of those who rebel against God, and we should walk where he calls us, accepting all the benefits he offers us, lest we be guilty of the ingratitude which the prophet here denounces and condemns in all who will not obey the gospel message.

That said, Isaiah shows that people do not deign to believe in Jesus Christ, since they see him as one who is marred. Our Lord Jesus, we know, is called 'a stumbling stone' and 'a rock of offence' (Rom. 9:32; 1 Pet. 2:8), because men strike hard against him. Yet he was given to us by God his Father for a quite different purpose: that we should be grounded in his grace, and that he should be the rock sustaining all of us. There is no one else who can give us solidity and support, only he. We ourselves are in a state of flux; hell yawns wide to swallow us up; we must rely for support on our Lord Jesus Christ. That is why he is said in the twenty-eighth chapter of Isaiah to have been set as a precious cornerstone on which God's temple would be built, a firm rock upholding the whole edifice (Isa. 28:16). The prophet also adds that in the kingdom of Judah and in the house of Israel he would be a rock of offence (Isa. 8:14).

In this passage our Lord Jesus is described as *a small shoot, a root springing from dry ground*, that is, from barren soil. He will be despised; no one will deign to look upon him; all will turn their faces from him; he will be an object of hate. That is why so few people will believe the gospel, for we always want to look good in our own eyes; we always want to shine. God, however, in seeking to redeem us, worked along very different lines. As Paul says, the world had no use for God's wisdom which revealed him as Creator, so that simply by looking at the heavens and the earth we might come to him (Rom. 1:19-20). God therefore changed his way of doing things: he employed a certain kind of folly in order to instruct us (1 Cor. 1:21). As I said earlier, we must all be taught by God's marvellous wisdom, which is manifest, high and low, to everyone in the world. Our minds, however, grew heavy and dull, which is why God employed folly of a sort by sending his only Son and by subjecting him to every kind of infirmity. The result was that, being born in a stable but rejected by the world, he remained a poor artisan throughout his life. Finally, we learn that everyone rose up against him, and with such fury that they loathed him, considering him to be the enemy of all; in the end they crucified him. This form of death was cursed by God (Deut. 21:23; Gal. 3:3). He was not only marred by men's blows, by their spitting and by the crown of thorns; he suffered the curse of being hung between two thieves, as if he were the most hated man that ever lived or was ever known to men. This was a frightful form of death, because it fell under the law's curse.

In these ways, then, he was marred, and it was offensive in men's eyes. Isaiah therefore insists that people will not believe the gospel because they cannot conceive that it is reasonable. They can on no account accept that God's Son, the Lord of glory, should have been the object of such abuse and shame. They cannot assent to God's eternal counsel which he purposed from eternity. Such is the prophet's meaning here.

Nevertheless, it is said that *he will grow up before him*. If, at the outset, he is insignificant, God will cause him to grow; he will appear as a small shoot springing from dry ground. Even so he will increase and will flower in all his glory, for God will see to it.

At this point the prophet reverts to the theme of our sin, in order to dispel the offence which we feel, thanks to our perverse disposition. When we see our Lord Jesus Christ thus marred, we might refuse to come to him. To avoid this, the prophet discloses the reason for it all. In truth, once we have acknowledged our sins and, at the same time, comprehended the fact of God's wrath, we will come to Jesus Christ, and our wish to be helped by him will make us all the keener to accept his death and passion. We will recognize that this is the necessary remedy for the evil within us. This, then, is the method which Isaiah employs here.

In comparing our Lord Jesus Christ to a young shoot and to a root in dry and barren ground, Isaiah's aim is to show that there will be small beginnings which no one will notice, which everyone in fact will laugh at and deride. Already in his eleventh chapter the prophet had compared our Lord to a small shoot, saying that it would come from the stem of Jesse, David's father (Isa. 11:1). Since at that time the royal house had been thrown down and had lost all greatness, the prophet declares that it will be as in former times. Jesse was a country man; the sons he had were oxherds and shepherds in the fields. His house was therefore obscure and of no repute. It was like the trunk of a tree which had been felled: people would trample upon it; it would be of no consequence.

Jesus Christ was thus, so to speak, a small shoot, but one which would grow so as to give shade to the whole world. Here again the prophet makes it clear that our Lord Jesus Christ was bound to be despised in the beginning. If this had not been said, we might have rightly taken offence on seeing that our Lord's coming was held in such contempt by men. Scripture, after all, had said that there would always be some who would sit on David's throne, and that their rule would prosper as long as there was sun and moon (2 Sam. 7:12-13; 1 Chron. 17:11-14; Psa. 89:35-37). Yet here the royal house has been practically annihilated and swept away. Who could imagine that the promise would be fulfilled in the person of Jesus Christ? There was no sign that things would be restored. So when it is said that David's house would fall and that sovereignty, sceptre and crown would be no more, and that men would feel almost ashamed to see such ruin and desolation—when all this is proclaimed by the prophets, here we have a promising way forward: our Lord Jesus Christ!

We should not be alarmed as if it were novel or strange that Jesus Christ should appear in so insignificant a fashion; nor was it only in this passage that the Holy Spirit spoke this way. Amos, we find, declares that God will again set up the throne which had earlier fallen (Amos 9:11), and this text is further cited in the fifteenth chapter of Acts, showing that our Lord Jesus Christ would begin to reign when God was pleased to repair what had been ruined (Acts 15:16). In particular it had been said that the kingdom would be trodden down, together with the royal crown, and that there would no longer be a leader who would wear it, until the Redeemer should come into the world (Isa. 6:10-12; 8:2-7; Jer. 22:5-8; Ezek. 22:17-22). All these things ought to strengthen our faith, so that we do not find it odd if Jesus Christ should have begun in so small a way.

Now in speaking of 'dry ground', the prophet means us to understand that no growth seemed likely for our Lord Jesus Christ, any more than for a tree in a desert where there is no moisture or anything else. He is therefore like a misshapen tree, unable to draw nourishment and moisture from the soil. This is how our Lord would first of all appear, the suggestion being that there would be no means here on earth which would allow him to increase, but that he would grow from a source on high, from the secret power of God his Father. The world would be of no help to him, for it contains only barrenness. And this is true not only of our Lord's birth; it relates also to the entire progress of the gospel.

That Jesus Christ was a young shoot is signified already by the fact that he found no place to make a home among men (Matt. 8:20; Luke 9:58). He was, as it were, shut out and banished from human company and grew up in such poverty that it is hard for us to recognize him as a man at all! Believers are thus already put on notice that Jesus Christ would be rejected and despised by men. The climax, however, was when he came forward to preach the gospel and to carry out the task committed to him by God his Father. People then began to ask: 'Is not this a carpenter's son? Don't we know how he was raised? In what school did he learn to become so great a teacher?' (Matt. 13:55-56). And his kinsmen, seeing how much he was hated, tried to convince him that he was out of his mind (Mark 3:21), and that he should be bound and stopped lest they all be stoned to death, for they realized that this hatred might turn against their own house. Last of all Jesus Christ was crucified, and the gospel seemed to be buried with him; in all likelihood all memory of it would be lost. Again, who would have thought that the apostles were able as they were to take the message of salvation forward? They were poor ignorant men, devoid of learning and untrained in holy Scripture; they had no skill or eloquence at all. Then too they were retiring men, whom others would not deign to hear, even if they spoke like angels!

What do we see in all of this, if not dry ground? Where is the ostentation and display, the elaborate preparations which might induce kings and rulers to yield to the gospel? On the contrary, see how swords are unsheathed and fires lit to prevent the message going forward. It is as if one small stick had been planted in dry, parched ground. Who would think that it would become a tree which would cover the whole world and where all could find refuge? Who could imagine such a thing, given such beginnings? The prophet Isaiah, therefore, has good grounds for declaring that people who are far too fond of outward show and loftiness will not deign to look upon Jesus Christ, but will treat him with contempt, since he is a mere shoot, a tiny twig springing from barren ground, from a place without water, moisture, nourishment or vigour.

Our attention is especially drawn to these things, lest they become an obstacle which might make us swerve aside or fall away, or which might stop us coming promptly to our Lord Jesus Christ. So when we are told how the gospel was to be proclaimed to the world, and when today we see the very same thing—that is, the church being only a handful of people who are regarded as a rabble!—and when, too, we are loathed by those who are riding high in the world, we should not lose heart, for we see just how our Lord Jesus Christ first appeared among men. And if today he still desires his kingdom to be preserved in the very same way, this should not stop us coming obediently to him.

We can be sure that, as Paul says, God's foolishness excels all human wisdom (1 Cor. 1:20), and that we should not be so arrogant as to oppose it. We should recognize that, as God chose to make his Son of no account, so too he willed to exalt him above the heavens. So let us regard as good and sound whatever he has decided in his counsel and let us willingly consent to it.

Consider again the words which say that, in spite of everything, 'he will grow up before him'. If, in our pride and petulance, we think that we can tread Jesus Christ underfoot and pin him to the ground, we are mistaken. He will increase despite our unbelief, malice, ingratitude and rebelliousness. Yes, he will increase in the sight of God, but also in the sight of all the faithful. They will worship him in full obedience, acknowledging that the supreme name given to him by God is of such worth that all will bow the knee before him. However, in saying that he will grow up before God, the prophet here is steering as it were a middle course between men who aim to overthrow the glory of our Lord and who endeavour to suppress it, and God his Father who will assist him, and who will ensure that nothing will keep him from attaining the fruit of the glory and majesty to which he has been called.

That is the natural sense of the words which speak of the Lord Jesus as a young shoot—which he is, when judged by outward appearances. It is as if he is in dry ground, because there is nothing in this world which can help him grow. Yet when all is said and done, he will grow up. How will he grow up? Before God. We should no longer be surprised, therefore, if people mock the message of the gospel and revile it: such is the pride which is found in unbelievers. When, however, we see the enemies of the gospel behaving so arrogantly, lifting up their horns against our Lord Jesus Christ and doing furious battle with him, let us look away; let us not be so foolish that we scorn the Son of God on the grounds that the blind and those possessed and bewitched by Satan do not praise him as he deserves. Instead, let us look to God and we will then be built up in our faith.

Since Jesus Christ grows up in the presence of God his Father, we rightly exalt him and pay him all that we owe. In a word, we should learn to rest wholly in God; then we may freely defy the world. And although the world takes no notice of God's word, we should not fail to give it our full obedience as we ought. Why so? Because God will mean more to us than a host of objectors who might dissuade us from coming to our Lord Jesus Christ. This is absolutely necessary today, for as I suggested earlier, we see the greatest people in the world and those reputed to be the wisest warring against the gospel; and those who boast of being the gospel's greatest allies, who are not content to call themselves Christians but who claim to be far superior to everyone else—these, I say, are allies of Satan, intent on crushing our Lord Jesus Christ and his word.

If, I say again, such things alarm us, attend to what we are told here. If people are so stubborn and hardened that they will not receive God's Son when he presents himself to them, we must defy them—yes, even if they are the greatest in the world. When compared with God they are mere rubbish! True, as things stand, they possess such majesty that it is as if everything must tremble beneath them. Once, however, we raise our minds to God and fix our eyes on him, most surely all the world's pomp and ceremony will no more impress us than a wisp of straw! Our faith should so rise that nothing that we see on earth should prevent us from accepting our Lord's authority over us. That is the lesson for us here. And although God may work in ways which are strange and beyond our comprehension, this ought to help us grow stronger in our faith. For if the gospel were preached by men of high repute, if kings and rulers were to submit to it, if it appealed to men of all conditions so that we might end up saying: 'We must hold fast to this! Here is heavenly truth which demands our assent!', and if everyone were favourably disposed and strove with might and main to observe it, it would be like rich, well cultivated soil, planted with trees and vines and sown with wheat—a place where everyone lent a hand and where no effort was spared. If ground like that was well cultivated, having rain in season and being well looked after; if, in a word, no effort was spared—what could be more natural? No one would see God's hand in any of that. As it is, today we see so much dissent and resistance which aim to repress the gospel; we see so many tongues for hire—nowadays throughout popery there are canting hypocrites who, like whores, hire themselves out in order to blaspheme against God and his word—not to mention similar villains among us, as we know. Again, we see what cruelty is meted out to God's poor children, and what new plots are hatched creating one decree after another in order to destroy all sound teaching. And then there is the mockery of the godless who put out their tongues and seek to blot out all religion. When we see all these things, we must conclude that God is still supreme, that his truth is victorious and that it comes from him.[2]

Our faith should thus be all the stronger when we see that there is nothing in this world which promotes the rule of Jesus Christ and the message of his gospel. Instead, everyone strives to hold it back, yet it continues to find an entry and to make itself felt. Now if we take offence at this we are condemned for our ingratitude, seeing that God calls us to himself and shows that he is the one who is at work. When the gospel flourishes in this way we should reckon it a miracle. That is how we are meant to put this teaching to good use.

Jesus Christ, we read, 'was marred'. There is more to be said about this phrase. Isaiah had already declared that, as a young shoot, he would be despised and rejected; no one would deign to look upon him, and there would be nothing in him that we might desire. It was necessary for him, then, as we said, to be reviled by all and to suffer shame as one cast out not only by men but by God. It would be wrong, it seems, to seek so desirable a thing as our salvation in one who looked so undistinguished! Nevertheless, here is a test that we must master if we would come to Jesus Christ. This is a necessity, because the Jews always expected an earthly Redeemer, and in their pride and avarice they thought that God could only show them mercy by amassing all the world's wealth, and by allowing them to live in ostentatious pleasure. Such was the Redeemer for whom they hoped.

[2] The preacher's point is that, despite formidable odds and the church's inevitable weakness, God's word continues to be preached, so that those with ears to hear are brought to repentance and faith. Paradoxically, the stronger the world's opposition, the more conspicuous is God's power to advance the gospel and to save. That the gospel still bears fruit, as Calvin goes on to say, must be regarded as a miracle of grace.

Yet God had reminded them that the Redeemer would be like a small shoot, rejected by the world. This warning was necessary not only for them but for us today. This continued to be a stumbling block even after the resurrection of our Lord, as Luke records when he describes how the Gentiles spoke of him with mockery (Acts 17:32). And the Jews, arming themselves with venom and ill-will, fell hard against this rock of offence. We see similar examples in our own day. It was necessary, therefore, that, as Scripture says, *in men's eyes the Son of God should have no form or comeliness that we might esteem him*. Even so, we should attend to what is said in the first chapter of John: 'In him was manifest the glory of the only Son of God' (John 1:14). Many, however, were blind and had no knowledge of this, so when the prophet speaks of Jesus Christ being marred, he means that we cannot, by our own natural understanding, discover that he was sent for our salvation, that he has complete power over life and death, and that he possesses righteousness, wisdom and holiness in all their fullness. We cannot, I repeat, imagine any such thing in our heads. What is signified here is that, although our Lord performed miracles which bore witness to his divine power, he was nevertheless marred, so that unbelievers could make no sense of it at all.

This prophetic passage has therefore always been fulfilled: there was no beauty in him which might draw people to him. Nor is it only his face that was meant: the prophet is speaking of his condition overall. Psalm 45 indeed declares that he will be fairest in beauty, above all humankind (Psa. 45:2). His beauty, however, was to be spiritual, as we already said, since it was the glory of the Son of God which was manifest in him—glory evident to those with eyes to see, and who were able to behold him. Accordingly, our Lord Jesus Christ surpassed all men in beauty, for God gave him unmistakable signs showing that he was the true and living image of God his Father. So while we have ample reason to extol our Lord, all this was hidden from the world. We should always, then, come back to this prophetic saying: all men turned their back on him; all closed their eyes to him as if he were an object of hate. 'What? Am I to seek my life in his death, my hope in him who could not save himself? Am I to seek my strength in one who proved so weak? What is the sense in that?' In a word, we all know, as experience makes only too clear, that because Jesus Christ humbled himself in death, our faith would totter if it could not find support somewhere else.

Whenever, therefore, it is a question of abiding in our Lord Jesus Christ, of turning to him for refuge and of placing our trust firmly in him, we might find ourselves saying: 'But he became as nothing! Was that not the end of him?' That is why we must turn back to what Isaiah tells us here: he was laid low in death, but God exalted him above every creature. This should lift our faith upward into heaven. Whatever happens, let us learn not to take offence when we see God's Son who was crucified, and who even today, in his members, is despised and abused in every way. Let us not, I say, fall away on that account, and let us always remain steadfast in the faith of his gospel.

It is because the fight is so difficult that Isaiah points us to the reason why our Lord suffered, for we can never rest in him until we are sure of the fruit which comes to us from his death and passion. Why is that? Because at first glance we might think it folly that the author of life should be a mortal man, that he should die—yes, die no simple death but a shameful one which was subject to God's curse—and that he should have been hung on the gallows like a thief. When we see these things, we would surely be seized by feelings of contempt, and we would never come to our Lord Jesus Christ. Yet the true remedy is to know why he died, how we may gain from his death and the benefits it confers on us. Then everything we find offensive will disappear.

To take an example: suppose I am troubled and anxious. When I see that God's only Son was trodden underfoot and loathed by men, I should pause to reflect. If I look first at myself and not at Jesus Christ, I will turn away and take no notice of him; but if I look from myself to him, what he suffered will have a wholesome taste for me. Again, if I remember that I am a poor sinner and that I have provoked God's wrath against me, making him both my adversary and my judge, then I will say: 'What can I do to settle things with God? Can I bring him something which will satisfy him for even the smallest wrong that I have done? Alas, no! If I traversed land and sea, could I find anything to make amends? Could the angels in heaven help me? Only Jesus Christ can appear on my behalf, only he can be my guarantor and go surety for me.' In this way our Lord's death and passion will cease to be folly to us. We must understand that, since we were accursed and had no means of finding favour in God's sight, since we had provoked him and made him our enemy, if Jesus Christ had not set us free, we would still be subject to Satan and his tyranny.

That, I say, is how we may begin to praise the infinite goodness of our God, to hate our sins and to feel ashamed of them. That too is how the offence we feel at the death and passion of our Lord will soon be wiped away, once we look within and carefully examine our sins, and once we realize that, since we are hateful to God, he had to come in the person of his Son to offer satisfaction, to make up for our iniquities and to reconcile us to himself.

These are the steps which the prophet outlines here. On the one hand, he says that Jesus Christ will have neither form nor face, nothing which might make us desire him. When, moreover, we see him from afar, we will feel appalled. But then, on the other hand, Isaiah adds: *He was afflicted for our sins*. It is as if he said, 'Poor blind souls, you think nothing of the Son of God.

All of you in your ingratitude shut the door to him, so that you cannot come close to him to obtain the salvation he brings you. It is because you have not acknowledged your sins and humbled yourselves. You have gone to sleep; you have grown senseless; you thrive on empty flattery. But if you consider your misery and your filth, you will be ashamed of your condition, and you will realize that the only remedy is for Jesus Christ to mediate between you, and to take upon himself all that made you enemies of God. He will have to be your surety, becoming, so to speak, a wretched sinner, while accepting all your burdens and bearing them himself. If you think upon these things, you will yield with good heart to the Son of God. Your idle thoughts will cease to be an obstacle, and you will no longer stumble at the fact that Jesus Christ made himself as nothing. You will see the condemnation which you deserved, and the atonement which was necessary to make up for it.'

We beheld him, says the prophet, *but we did not esteem him*. What this reveals is that Jesus Christ would be scorned and rejected, not by a few but by the greater number, by the very people who were especially close to him. The prophet, placing himself among those who would reject our Lord, looks upon his people, the Jews, among whom he was born. He seeks to show that this was the common belief: Jesus Christ would be spurned by almost everyone.

We are therefore all the better equipped not to bind ourselves to the opinions of mere men. When we see unbelievers not only in their hundreds but in crowd upon crowd, heavily armed and coming in their millions, and when out of every hundred only three or four are found who quietly obey our Lord Jesus Christ—when we see that, let us nevertheless hold fast to him. That is the message of this verse.

Nowadays we like to count heads. There are many frail souls who tell themselves, 'Look, only a handful of people believe the gospel. If they excelled in number, I would gladly yield. But what is the point of joining so small a number and abandoning the great majority?' Hence to put paid to such objections, Isaiah declares that not just five or ten, but, overall, almost everyone will refuse to obey our Lord Jesus Christ. Doubtless he means to criticize the Jews particularly, for already the eighth chapter which we cited before speaks of our Lord as a rock of offence to both houses, that is, to Abraham's line (Isa. 8:14). This people who above all others belonged to God ought, it appears, to have acknowledged their Redeemer. To whom, after all, was Jesus Christ promised, if not to the Jews? For he is said to be the servant of the circumcision, in order to fulfil the promises which the patriarchs received (Rom. 15:8).

Thus, the Jews should have been quite accustomed to our Lord Jesus Christ, even before he appeared in the world, and they should have had no difficulty welcoming him. Instead, it is said that he was rejected by them, that is, by the builders who were the leaders of the people and who had responsibility for them (Psa. 118:22). We continue to see the same today, for it is not only the Turks and the heathen who reject Jesus Christ, but those who usurp the name 'Christianity' and who falsify it. Even those who profess the gospel are often worldly people, despisers of God, villains who would love to do away with the message of salvation; and if they do hold on to it, it is only in order to avoid public shame.

Whatever the case, Jesus Christ was destined to be despised and rejected. If this had not been foretold, we would most probably have been shaken in our faith. As it is, this saying of Isaiah's should be like a staff which supports us, or like a firm rock, since we see that everyone comes up hard against our Lord Jesus Christ. Some defy him and rise up furiously against him and his teaching; others deride him and, scorning all religion, put out their tongues. It is then that we must persevere, being steadfast in our faith. True, it is greatly to be desired that we should behold Jesus Christ from afar and should yield obedience to him who is the true mirror and model of all holiness. In any case, the more we see the world rejecting him, the stronger our faith should be. How indeed can we discern that he is the world's Redeemer? We must consider all that is said about him by the prophets. There we find the true mirror in which we may behold the glory of God's only Son. These are the genuine witnesses sent by God from heaven to point to what our Redeemer would be—one rejected by all, one against whom all would rebel.

Since this is so, let these be the terms on which we receive him, and let us not doubt that when we seem likely to be completely overwhelmed and trodden down by arrogant and reckless evil-doers, God will nevertheless exalt our Lord Jesus Christ; he will also reinforce our faith by his Holy Spirit, making it victorious in the end. And just as Jesus Christ vanquished the devil, and just as Satan and his henchmen will finally be made his footstool (Psa. 110:1), so too he will cause us to triumph with him, and to walk over those who now persecute us, who rise up in wrath against us and who defy and despise our Lord.

Now let us cast ourselves down before the majesty of our good God, acknowledging our faults and begging him so to make us feel them that we sigh and groan. May we, having truly humbled ourselves, come to our Lord Jesus Christ, knowing that he is our perfect refuge. And because he was afflicted by God his Father for our sins, let us fix every thought and feeling on him. May we feel true distress at having provoked God's wrath, so that we come to hate ourselves and our sins, until we are wholly cleansed of them. May he uphold us all the while, and may we not doubt his continuing favour toward us, since Jesus Christ not only suffered once and for all to blot out our sins, but daily offers us forgiveness when we look to him for what we ourselves lack.

3

STRICKEN FOR OUR INIQUITIES

Truly he bore our weaknesses and carried our sorrows. Yet we esteemed him stricken by God and afflicted. [5] *He was stricken for our iniquities and afflicted for our sins; the chastisement of our peace was upon him, and by his wounds we are healed.* [6] *We have all strayed like sheep; each has followed his own way, and the Lord has laid all our iniquities on him* (Isa. 53:4-6).

WHEN we contemplate all of God's works throughout the world, Scripture says that he should be praised according to his loftiness and greatness. When, on the other hand, we consider the person of our Lord Jesus Christ, we must learn to glorify God in his humility.

There are two ways in which we may praise God. First, when he displays his infinite goodness, righteousness and power in all that he has created and done. He also deserves to be extolled for ordering and directing everything. Not that we can confer greatness upon him, but Scripture speaks this way so that we may learn to lift our minds on high, above the world, when we seek to glorify God as he deserves. A second way of praising God is this: our Lord Jesus Christ, in whom dwells all fullness of deity, not only humbled himself for our salvation but made himself as nothing, not refusing even to suffer the pangs of death, but entering as it were into hell itself. In this God deserves to be glorified even more than in his greatness, which is conspicuous throughout the world. We touched on this point yesterday, but because the prophet is continuing his theme, we must keep this end in view: while the faithless are appalled to see that our Lord was afflicted by the hand of God his Father, and take offence so that they depart from him, we ourselves should be all the more encouraged to seek him out. We ought to delight in his love, for he did not spare himself but chose to bear all our burdens and to relieve us of them.

Given, then, that for our sake our Lord Jesus Christ made this exchange, paying the full price for our debts that we might be free of them; and given that he was willing to be condemned for us, and as it were in our very person, so that we might be absolved, this should surely draw us to him, and so enthuse us that it is here we find our rest.

He was afflicted by the hand of God, declares Isaiah, but all for our iniquities. If we give no thought to God's judgment, the death and passion of Jesus Christ will be of no use to us, and we can receive no benefit from them. The main thing is that we must settle our differences with God: he is our enemy until our transgressions have been buried, for he who is the source of all righteousness cannot love iniquity. He must thus be our judge as long as he imputes our sins to us and considers who we are. When, however, Jesus Christ comes between us and offers to act on our behalf, then we are acceptable to God, since atonement has been made for all our sins. The condemnation suffered by our Lord Jesus Christ cannot have been in vain. The fact is that he committed no offence; he was in no way guilty. He was therefore condemned in order to absolve us, which is why he is called the Lamb without blemish (1 Pet. 1:19).

He is called 'Lamb' because he was offered up as a sacrifice. He was without blemish in order to show that he bore all our burdens, which is why his blood is said to be our cleansing (1 John 1:7), for we are unclean and full of defilement until we have been washed by the blood of Jesus Christ. The prophet is right, therefore, to recall us to God's judgment, when he says that our Lord was afflicted because it was necessary for him to bear our condemnation. In short, whenever we think of how our Lord's death and passion have benefited us, let us each look to the judgment seat of God, where we will find that we are all guilty.

How severe, then, is God's judgment! How awful is his retribution! It is enough to swallow all of us up and to destroy us. Yet because God did not spare our Lord Jesus Christ but laid upon him the severity of his judgment, and because our Lord himself was there on our behalf, acting as surety for us, we can be certain that now God will no longer pursue us, call us to account or punish us according to our transgressions and demerits.

It is of course true that God felt exactly the same toward his Son as when he said: 'This is my beloved Son in whom I delight. Listen to him' (Matt. 3:17; 17:5). Indeed, as Paul declares in the first chapter of Ephesians, we could not be pleasing to God for the sake of his only Son, if he were not first and foremost, and supremely, the beloved Son (Eph. 1:6). Nevertheless, this does not alter the fact that we are only acquitted because of the severity which God visited upon our Lord Jesus Christ. He loved him, yet he was willing to afflict him for our transgressions. God did not consider our Lord's righteousness, integrity and perfection: he treated him as if he were the embodiment of all who sin. Our Lord was therefore burdened with all our offences and iniquities—not that he himself was guilty, but God chose to impute everything to him, to hold him accountable and to require him to pay the price. This is how we are to read the prophet's words, when he says that Jesus Christ not only was crucified by the hands of men, but appeared before the judgment seat of God, answering in our name and humbly bearing the burden which we deserved.

The prophet thus declares that *he bore our sins and transgressions*. Peter makes the same point when he speaks of the cross as a tree (1 Pet. 2:24), showing that the type of death which the Son of God suffered was clear and visible evidence that our sins were laid on him, for the law had said, 'Cursed is he who hangs upon the tree' (Deut. 21:23). Jesus Christ was therefore hung, so that we might know that it was in and for us that he was cursed. Paul says the same when speaking to the Galatians (Gal. 3:13), exhorting us to see God's wonderful goodness, and our Lord Jesus Christ's boundless love, in his willingness not only to die for us but to endure an accursed death, so that we might obtain God's blessing. And although our iniquities appal us, just as God's judgment does when we know how hateful we are to him when we offend him, and when our conscience pricks us, nevertheless we can be sure that he will pardon our sins and will welcome us as his beloved children, righteous and without reproach, since our curse was ended on the cross where our Lord hung. This point is added by Isaiah by way of a more detailed explanation.

The prophet goes further still, declaring that he was afflicted *because the chastisement*—or *amendment*—*of our peace was upon him*. Isaiah here is adding nothing new, but he explains himself in a more direct and personal way. We are to understand that our Lord Jesus Christ was struck and smitten by the hand of God, in order to free us of our burdens. He therefore bore the punishment which was owed to us, a punishment which made for peace. Some, it is true, believe that Jesus Christ was punished on our behalf because we were so dull and stupid that no one thought of humbling himself before God; we were blind to our failings.[1] The prophet's natural meaning, however, is that a different way was needed to give us peace with God and to reconcile us to him.

I said before that, since God is judge of all the world, he rightly hates us and regards us all with abhorrence, for, as will soon become clear, what do we bring from our mother's womb, and what wealth do we amass in all our years of life? We continually provoke God's wrath, as if we had conspired with Satan to fan the flames still more. We deserve, then, to be cast off by God and to be hated by him. He for his part is armed with wrath against us; he is bound to be opposed to us, for we fight against him and do all-out battle with him. We sin against all that is right. God must on that account rise up in judgment against us, for we know that his office is to uphold equity and justice. And since he sees us full of iniquity and corruption, rebellious through and through, he must put forth his arm and show that, because we are his enemies, he must repay us with like coin.

It follows, then, that we have no peace, and our consciences are always reproaching us. And although we want simply to slumber in our self-satisfaction, God does not fail to prick and goad us, so that, despite ourselves, we are conscious only of evil and ingratitude within. It is thus impossible for God to have mercy on us, and for us to be sure of finding favour in his sight, until amendment has been made. Not that God desires vengeance after the manner and fashion of men. A person motivated by anger will demand that wrongs be righted, and that, if he is to be avenged, some penalty or punishment be imposed. God has no passions of this kind. Even so, to help us feel greater abhorrence of our sins and to teach us to detest them, he chooses to show us his righteousness and the severity of his judgment. If he forgave

[1] Calvin's reference is unclear. Max Engammare (*SC* IV/1:74) suggests that Calvin may have in mind Sebastian Münster, who in a note to his *Biblia hebraica* expresses an idea close to the one Calvin is criticizing.

us without the need for Jesus Christ to intercede for us and to go surety for us, we would take no notice. All of us would shrug it off and would seize the chance to take still greater liberties. When, however, we see that God did not spare his only Son but treated him with such extreme severity that in his body he felt all the pains that it is possible to feel, and that in his soul he endured profound distress so that he cried, 'My God, my God, why have you forsaken me?' (Matt. 27:46)—when we learn of all these things, unless we are harder than stones we are bound to shiver and to feel fear and dread, being utterly put to shame.

It is impossible for us not to hate our sins and iniquities, since they provoke God's wrath against us. This is why it was necessary that the chastisement of our peace should be upon Jesus Christ. It is this that allows us to find favour in the sight of God his Father, favour which comes when we settle our differences with God. Today, then, we have boldness and freedom to call upon God as our Father, even though he might rightfully be our enemy and might hate us as we are by nature.

The prophet's meaning is thus clear, when he declares that our Lord was afflicted by the hand of God and was so marred that all turned away from him, not deigning to look at him on account of his disfigurement. He also explains that this was because God's wrath burned hot against us, and that he was armed to crush us and to wipe us out, until reconciliation should be made. By what means was this achieved? It was all because God willed in his unmerited grace to pardon our faults, his only Son, however, being the price paid for our redemption.

Here we must note that because our Lord Jesus Christ suffered condemnation, we are acquitted and absolved; our offences are buried and no longer count before God. When we speak of the forgiveness of sins, it is not that God writes them off as if we had paid for them and thus had given him satisfaction. No, God is being uniquely generous. And although we are guilty before him, he forgets it all and receives us in mercy because, as the prophet says, he casts our sins into the depths of the sea (Mic. 7:19). Forgiveness was not, however, free, so far as Jesus Christ was concerned: it cost him most dear. If we weigh up just how bitter, cruel and shameful was the death he endured, and how deep the anguish which he suffered in his soul when he was called before the judgment seat of God his Father to bear our condemnation—if we carefully reflect on all of this, we will see that our Lord Jesus Christ paid an extraordinary price to acquit us of our offences. That is why today we are free of them.

This is something we need to understand, for the devil has always tried to obscure this truth, because it is the foremost article of our faith. From the beginning of the world God wished us to plead for pardon for sin by offering sacrifice to him. Why? To demonstrate that we could not hope for pardon from him except through sacrifice and the shedding of blood. Everybody, then, when they sacrificed, confessed that they could not draw near to God unless they were redeemed, and that cleansing from sin and iniquity was, or would be made, by our Lord Jesus Christ.[2]

Nevertheless, both Jews and Gentiles continually trusted in their own merits, imagining that they could always offer God satisfaction. In this way the devil turned poor sinners away from Jesus Christ and from the payment he made by his death and passion. It is still like that today with the papists. They admit that we have full remission of sins by our Lord's death and passion, but only, they believe, for sins prior to baptism. Children, they maintain, have received grace from God such that he forgives original sin in baptism by virtue of Jesus Christ's death and passion. Once, however, we have been baptized, they say that if we then sin, Jesus Christ is not enough to make us

[2] The ubiquity of blood-sacrifice is, for Calvin, proof that atonement for sin is not only a divine requirement but a necessary part of natural religion. Before Christ's advent, the exact manner of atonement was, of course, known only to God, although foreshadowed by the sacrifices enjoined by the law.

acceptable to God and to ensure that the memory of our sins is blotted out. We for our part must also make compensation. That is why they have dreamed up their works of supererogation, such as trotting about on pilgrimages, having lots of masses sung, and other such devilish devices. If we ask the papists why they go off to see the pouting face of some grim statuette, why they fast on such-and-such a day, why they erect a church or have some mass sung, 'It's to obtain redemption in God's sight,' they say. 'Since we recognize our sins, we are trying to offer satisfaction for them, so that we will be cleared of our debts before God.'[3]

See how the power of the death and passion of our Lord Jesus Christ is swept aside! In doing their devotions, the papists cannot take one step without blaspheming against God, openly denying the death and passion of our Lord and rushing headlong into the pit of hell! That is where their devilish devotions, which they call 'good', lead them. We ought, then, to pay close attention when it is said that the chastisement of our peace was upon our Lord Jesus Christ. It is through him that God has been appeased and reconciliation made. He took upon himself all the world's evils and iniquities. So when we consider the kind of people we are, we should always be afraid, since God is our adversary and our judge. In the second place, however, we should make up our minds that there is no way in heaven or on earth to settle our differences with God except through the price which Jesus Christ himself paid, and by which he made satisfaction—that is, by his death and passion. Is this true of us? Then let us

[3] The Roman Catholic doctrine of baptism, confirmed by the Council of Trent in 1547, held that although the sacrament cancels the effects of original sin and of personal sins committed before baptism, the penalty attaching to sins committed after baptism remained. The remedy for such sins was the sacrament of penance, involving contrition, confession, absolution and satisfaction. While forgiveness belonged to God, satisfaction was conceived as a means of making amends for wrongs done, and of strengthening the penitent against future temptation. Special merit attached to works of supererogation—works done over and above the strict demands of the law. Cf. *Inst.* III.4.25-27, 29-30; III.14.12-15.

come before God with boldness and with heads held high. Not that we should not always come humbly, being ashamed of our wretchedness. Still, this should not stop us from freely calling upon God as our Father and from boasting that we are counted righteous in his sight, since all of our debts have been paid. We are absolved by virtue of the condemnation borne by our Lord Jesus Christ. That is the lesson to be drawn from this passage.

The next thing the prophet says is this: *By his wounds we are healed*. It is true that we do not visibly recognize our failings because hypocrisy blindfolds us and because of our all-prevailing pride. We thus deceive ourselves and make believe that God remains answerable to us. Or else we are so dim-witted that we think we will never be held to account. Whatever the case, Isaiah here shows that, but for the wounds which Jesus Christ bore, there is only death in us: to him alone we must look for healing. If we would really experience the fruits of our Lord's death and passion, picture the many faults which are rooted in our nature as so many mortal wounds and maladies, even though they may not be readily apparent.

Tell me, when an abscess occurs inside the human body, in the area of the stomach perhaps or in the bowels, will it not be worse than if it was visible and so could be lanced? If someone thought that he was healthy as long as he could not see his illness, he would have to be mad, bereft of reason! Our illnesses are bound to be all the deadlier the more secret they are. And as well as our inner failings whose roots are hidden within us, there are the wrongs we commit every day, which amply prove that by nature we are wilful and accursed and are completely perverted. Accordingly, because we are wholly defiled—spiritual lepers, made rotten by our iniquities—what are we to do? What cure can there be? Shall we look to the angels in heaven? Alas, they cannot help. We must come instead to our Lord Jesus Christ, who consented to be marred from the top of his head to the soles of his feet, to be covered in wounds, scourged stroke after stroke, crowned with thorns, nailed and tied to the cross and pierced in his side. That is how we are protected; there is our true medicine which should be sufficient for us. Here is where we should fix our minds, knowing that nowhere else can we find inner rest. We will have endless trouble and torment unless Jesus Christ comforts us and allays God's wrath against us. When we are certain of these things, God gives us cause to sing his praises, whereas before we could only groan and feel dismay. This is what the prophet wants us to remember.

Matthew, in his eighth chapter, cites this verse, declaring that our Lord Jesus Christ healed all who were sick (Matt. 8:17): he gave light to the blind, enabled the lame to walk, restored hearing to the deaf, lifted up the paralytic and those who were half dead, and drove out demons from the body. 'This,' he writes, 'shows how right the prophet Isaiah was to say that he bore our weaknesses.' It is certain, however, that the prophet is not speaking of bodily illnesses here. It might therefore seem that the Evangelist misinterpreted Isaiah's testimony; but while Jesus Christ is said to have healed obvious sicknesses, Matthew seeks to take us higher up, allowing us to contemplate, in figurative form, the reason why our Lord came into the world. Thus when we hear that our Lord gave strength to the paralytic, and similarly raised the dead and healed all manner of illness, we should understand that, visibly, according to our ignorance and infirmity, he is seen to be our spiritual physician. We are thus taught, as I said before, that all the faults to which we are inclined are so many defilements of our soul. And just as in the body there are harmful humours and other such things, that is, secret maladies, so too there are in our souls. Because these are full of evil in God's sight, they also need a physician. Who then is he? We will find him neither in heaven nor on earth, unless it be the one who has been given to us by the heavenly Father: our Lord Jesus Christ.

If we do not know that the Lord Jesus brought healing to our souls, we should look to the imagery employed here, concerning the blind who receive their sight. Without doubt in our souls there is only blindness and stupidity. Then too, Jesus Christ caused the dumb to speak. Now how do we use our tongue if not for evil, until Jesus Christ restores it to its proper use? We are profoundly deaf, since God's word finds no way in to us. Our hearing needs to be restored, again by our Lord Jesus Christ. In short, when we combine the things that Matthew describes with what the prophet seeks to say—the fact, that is, that we are full of corruption and mischief, with not a drop of health in us and with our souls brimful of deadly evils, but that our Lord Jesus Christ has delivered us from them all and grants us healing when we come to him—when, I say, we combine one with the other, we will see that, unless we come for refuge to our Redeemer, we must forever wallow in our sins and wretchedness, and rot and perish in them.

At this point Isaiah declares that *we have all turned aside; each one has gone his own way*. The prophet's purpose here is to touch us more directly, to the quick. As I mentioned yesterday, we are not conscious of our need to be healed by Jesus Christ until each of us has carefully examined his condition and discovered how he really is. Why are we so cold and unconcerned when we are told to come to Jesus Christ? It is because we have no understanding; we are more or less senseless. Now we know that there are drunkards steeped in insobriety who indulge themselves endlessly until they gnash their teeth and can do no more. If we mention physicians to them, they do nothing but joke, shake their heads and laugh at the idea of a cure. There is, however, no worse drunkenness than the mindless folly of all poor sinners, until, that is, they realize what it means to have God as their adversary.

All of us freely give ourselves to evil; we disdain the death and passion of our Lord Jesus Christ and give no thought to them.

The prophet, therefore, in order to wake us up and to make us more eager for the blessing brought to us by Jesus Christ, rightly insists that we have all gone astray. Now as I said, men in their worldliness despise God's judgment, besides which there are others who are puffed up with foolish arrogance. So there are two types of people who cannot benefit from the infinite grace obtained for us by the Son of God. Some think of themselves as righteous, possessing meritorious works by which they can account to God. Hence we see in popery pious frauds who not only fancy that they have paid God his dues, but who also sell portion of their merits as if they had a surplus of them! And people are only too happy to be given a share in the perfection and holiness of those who are in an angelic state! People like this do not believe they need the death and passion of Jesus Christ. Of course, through half-closed lips, they profess they do need them, but it is the opposite that we see. They trade their merits in the marketplace, putting them up for sale, so that others will rely on them and put their trust in such a profanation.[4]

All these popish bigots—men and women—are so many horns raised up against God himself. They are forever swollen with pride, so that they say, 'Look, unless I acquired merits, what would be the point of performing so many good devotions, of having had so many masses sung, of having mumbled so many prayers, of having run from altar to altar, of having singled out such-and-such a saint for veneration, and of having observed such-and-such a feast-day?' In a word, they are always driven by the hellish and accursed belief that they can put God in their debt. These are the delusions with which Satan tricks them, so that they are incapable of tasting how our Lord's death and passion might benefit them.

[4] Calvin's target here is the doctrine, so energetically assailed by Luther forty years earlier, that the church possesses, by virtue of Christ and the saints' superabundant merits, a treasury for the living and the dead which can be dispensed in the form of indulgences, usually for a fee. That the church's treasury supplemented, but did not replace, the value of individual good works, is clear from the next paragraph.

The others of whom I spoke do not trust in their own merits. Like drunkards, like immoral or dissolute men, they do not say, 'We are like little angels. We have lived good lives and have been fervent in our devotions.' No, they joke, as I said, thinking that they can escape God's hand by their mockery and contempt. That is why the prophet calls to all of us here and says to us: 'Consider, poor people, just who you are, and how God has revealed to you his mercy in his Son, our Lord Jesus Christ. You have all strayed; you are all lost, like sheep.' Now in speaking of 'us all', Isaiah means to place himself among our number. The fact is that the Jews were necessarily included in the general condemnation of all humanity, although it seemed to them that they should be exempt. In their foolish pride they believed that because God had adopted and chosen them, they were better than the rest. Here, however, the prophet enfolds them in the same eternal death, until they seek as their remedy deliverance in Jesus Christ.

We are all, therefore, included in this condemnation, so that the word 'all' is used to rule out any exception. It is as if Isaiah were saying, 'No one, to the very last man, should boast that he is righteous before God and has no need of the remedy which I now set before you. He who is most perfect and most holy in men's eyes is guilty in God's sight.' So the prophet's meaning is clear.

Nevertheless he is not content to have made that point. He now adds that 'each has gone his own way'. Why does he repeat himself by passing from 'all' to 'each'? It is because when we are all alike condemned, we are not so strongly or so keenly moved as we should be. True, we must admit our guilt when we are told that, among men, there is no one who is righteous. So we read elsewhere in the Psalms that God looked but could not find a single person who was not riddled with sin (Psa. 14:2-3). The same Psalm speaks of those who are upright and who are held in high and exceptional repute, as well as of those who are most in error. Yet all are said to have gone astray: not one was found who was not wholly corrupt before God. Holy Scripture is full of this teaching. Paul amply expounds it in the third chapter of Romans, citing all the verses in the Psalms and prophets which speak of men defiled, in whom is only treachery and wickedness, men full of cruelty, poison and violence, deceit and robbery, and whose throat is an open grave (Rom. 3:10-18). Having said all this, Paul adds that everyone is included without exception, until God changes them and renews them by his Holy Spirit.

Now when this message is preached to us, we should all hang our heads, for we would be ashamed and horrified to think that we might answer God back. In any case, what would we gain from all our arguing? We must, despite ourselves, come to see that it is not without good reason that we stand condemned, for God is our judge. Nevertheless, each of us will return home unmoved: what has been said will hardly touch us at all. We will of course all admit to being sinners; there is no one, we will say, who is not guilty in God's sight. But do we feel our faults so that we cease to love them, and are led instead to seek the grace of our Lord Jesus Christ and to deny ourselves? Not at all! It is enough if we confess for form's sake that we are all sinners. What is worse, we will often see people boldly making excuses when they are accused of doing wrong and are convicted of their error. 'Oh yes,' they say, 'we are all sinners.' Evildoers who have blasphemed against God's name or who have done some foul, abominable deed, if taken to task will first of all deny it. They can never be made to confess except when forced to do so. But what if they are shown to be at fault? 'It's true,' they reply, 'we are all sinners.' In other words, you are wicked hypocrites, you are mocking God!

We see therefore that given the commonality of sin, there are many who look for some excuse, so that their villainy is not acknowledged as it should be. That is why the prophet, as well as saying that all have strayed, adds the words, 'Each, each one.' It is as if he said, 'Do not consider what the human race is like overall. Let each one draw apart, think about himself and examine just who he is.' It is then that we are touched by the fact of God's judgment and are led to true humility. We really feel our plight and are brought to repentance when each of us speaks to himself in secret, as it were.

For the rest, when Isaiah declares that we have each turned to his own way, he teaches us in the first place what we are like when we behave as we please, according to our own reason and judgment. This is another point well worth noting, because we know there are some who are so foolish that no one can convince them that, in doing as they like, they are rushing to destruction. Others are so mindless and greedy that they cannot see that, unless God comes to their rescue, they are throwing themselves into the depths of hell.

Today, when we censure the papists from the word of God and convince them of their error, they reply, 'Oh, leave me alone. I'm going on as usual, whatever you say!' 'But you are heading for the devil. That's where you'll end up if you keep on as you are.' 'Is that so? I make my devotions. They are good and proper. How could God reject them?' 'Yes, but the prophet Isaiah is here speaking precisely of each man's devotions. And did not the Holy Spirit, who spoke at that time by his mouth, not know that you would become a pious fraud, full of pride and poison; that you would behave any way you pleased and would try to invent your own ways of serving God, believing that you were doing good by worshipping idols? Those are the devotions you make!'

Did not the Holy Spirit know all about these evils? Consider what he says, 'Each has gone his own way.' That is, each has taken the road to hell; by continuing on as usual, each has run headlong to perdition. Such are the ways of men.

What this verse teaches us, then, is that we must rid ourselves of our stupid arrogance. In doing as we please, in doing what we think is reasonable, we are like those who have conspired with Satan to cast themselves into his nets. This teaching should therefore help us to correct all presumptuousness, so that we allow only the Holy Spirit and God's word to rule and direct us. Likewise, we should observe that although we know what is right, we are nevertheless addicted to evil. Why? Because our every impulse is to rebel against God. We understand that we must keep from evil, but we are driven to it, not by constraint but by our own wilfulness, which is so ingrained in us that its fruit clearly reveals what is its root.

Notice first of all, then, that we do not have the discernment to be able to walk aright. There is only one way which meets with God's approval, and which will lead us to salvation: it is when Jesus Christ takes us into his care, and when we become the sheep of his flock and follow him as our shepherd. Notice also that all our feelings are defiled and that we seek evil rather than good, until our Lord Jesus Christ sets us right, remaking us and giving us a true desire to obey him. That is the prophet's lesson for us here.

We are thus led to conclude that all who run about in circles turn away from our Lord Jesus Christ. Isaiah insists that there was not a patriarch or prophet, not a single one of all the holy fathers and martyrs, who did not need to be reconciled to God by the death and passion of Jesus Christ. If Abraham, the father of the faithful, if David, a mirror of all righteousness, and if others like them, such as Job and Daniel who were called mirrors of all holiness and perfection—if these, I say, were poor sheep lost and straying until gathered in by Jesus Christ, what, alas, can be said of us? So when we come looking to them as our mediators and hope that, through them, we may escape the perdition in which we now are, is this not proof that we are utterly ungrateful to our Lord Jesus Christ? And that we are completely out of our minds when we come as beggars to those who also need to look for help to our Lord's death and passion? If necessity forces us to seek a remedy, we must go to him to whom the faithful in every age have turned for refuge. No one is exempt, neither St Peter, St Paul, the Virgin Mary, nor anyone at all.

Accordingly, let us learn to come to this source and fountain-head, so that we may draw from him all that we lack. Our Lord Jesus Christ has sufficient to satisfy all of us. We should not fear that the fullness of grace which he possesses will ever run dry; he will give his part and portion to each one who comes seeking it in him. Let us come boldly, then, to our Lord Jesus Christ, who will amply supply us all. Anyone, however, who strays to this side or that will get no help from the remedy which God offers. He rejects God so far as he is able; his thanklessness prevents him from enjoying the grace which is set before him. We ourselves will have all the less excuse, because this message is daily preached to us. God was not content to have sent his only Son once and once only, to have exposed him to death and to have stricken him in his wrath, although he loved him as his only Son. For although he appeared to want to destroy him and treated him with all severity, he was always the well-loved Son, as we have said: it was all done in order to absolve us. God, I say, was not content with that. Each and every day he lays this treasure before us for us to enjoy. He tells us that Jesus Christ whose side was pierced has today opened up his heart so that we may be sure of the love he bears us. And just as his arms were nailed to the cross, so now he holds them out wide in order to draw us to himself. He wants all these things to be for our benefit, and having shed his blood he would have us immerse ourselves in it.

God, then, gently invites us to come, and Jesus Christ sets before us the fruit of his death and passion, showing us how fresh is his blood, as the apostle says in the letter to the Hebrews

(Heb. 10:20). For this is not blood which dries or fails: because he sanctified himself by his heavenly power, his blood is ever fresh. That is how the apostle describes it. We should therefore know that its power is not diminished and that it is still fully effective, just as it was in the beginning. All of us, then, should come in obedience to our Lord Jesus Christ, and having confessed our wretchedness and our shame, we should not doubt that he is able to supply such a cure that we can finally be sure that God has received us as his own children, and that he counts us righteous and blameless, whereas before we were abhorrent to him.

That is the lesson we must bear in mind. Today, when we see some who laugh and jeer, and others who rise up in pride and presumption, thinking that they can satisfy God by their own righteousness, let us cease from such blasphemies, and with true faith and repentance let us seek our Lord Jesus Christ; and when we feel the weight of our intolerable load, let us set our heart on giving him our obedience.

Now let us cast ourselves down before the majesty of our good God, acknowledging our faults and asking him so to make us feel them that we may groan all the days of our lives, and be led to turn to him, lest we wander far in our foolish, wicked thinking. And since we know that every blessing and all that concerns our salvation is found in our Lord Jesus Christ, may it please our God to direct us wholly to him, and to keep us in such faith that we never fall away. May he, by the power of his Holy Spirit, so work in our hearts that, conscious that we have free forgiveness for our sins, we may be made to see how dearly it cost his only Son, and may this stir us up to exalt him all the more. And since full healing must be sought in him alone, may he daily cleanse us of our faults and failings, until he brings us to that perfection for which we should strive as long as we live.

4

A LAMB TO THE SLAUGHTER

He was punished and afflicted, but he did not open his mouth; he was led like a lamb to the slaughter, and as a lamb before his hearers is dumb, so he did not open his mouth. [8] *He was taken up from anguish and from judgment, and who will tell of his generation? He was cut off from the land of the living, and he suffered the wounds which were owed to my people* (Isa. 53:7-8).

THE prophet, having first declared that, if we are to savour our Lord's death and passion, each of us must look to himself and his failings, now adds that Jesus Christ was not compelled to suffer as he did: he did it of his own free will. Without it we would not be justified; there would be no reconciliation between God and us if Jesus Christ had not, by his obedience, made up for our transgressions.

If the death of God's Son had been forced upon him, and if he had not yielded to it of his own accord, it would not have been a sacrifice capable of blotting out our sins. Paul refers to this when he writes that our rebelliousness has been cancelled by one man's obedience (Rom. 5:19). What was it that made God our enemy, and that makes him so today, if not the fact that we continually offend him? He created us so that he might enjoy us in all tranquillity; but when we refuse to bear his yoke, he is bound to abhor us and to disown us as his creatures, and rightly so. That, then, is why Scripture says that not only was Jesus Christ punished for our faults and iniquities, but that *he did not open his mouth*. He made no protest; instead, knowing that he had been appointed for this very thing, and that such was the eternal counsel of God his Father, he was obedient even to death.

Hence, if we would better appreciate the power of the death and passion of the Son of God, let each of us think of the many ways in which we have sinned against God's will and righteousness. We will find that we do not cease to war with him, as if we mean deliberately to defy him. It is not surprising, therefore, if we needed a remedy like this, namely that the Son of God should render obedience in our place, in order to bury the memory of our rebelliousness.

It is true that our Lord Jesus Christ spoke in the presence of Pilate, his judge (Matt. 27:11; Mark 15:2; Luke 23:3; John 18:34, 36-37). He did so, however, not in order to escape death. Indeed, he offered himself up to it, nor did he seize the chance to be acquitted: it was most necessary for him to be condemned for our sake. Isaiah is right to say that *he was as one who is dumb, like a sheep or a lamb*, thus thinking of the symbolism of the ancient sacrifices. When we are told about our Lord's death and passion, we must regard it as a sacrifice by which God was appeased, given that this was the only way, as we said before, that sins can be effaced in God's sight. Sure enough, when under the law men sought pardon for their wrongs, sacrifice had always to be added. They could offer nothing by way of compensation, but God had shown them that it was sufficient if they relied on the promise of the Redeemer. To convince the Jews that Jesus Christ was destined to fulfil all that the law in those times symbolized, the name 'Lamb' is ascribed to him, and the prophet includes everything in this one class, meaning that in his death and passion Jesus Christ would first sweep all our iniquities away, since he would submit to the will of God his Father. And second, he would be sacrificed as a lamb, so that through his shed blood we would be washed and cleansed of all our stains.

Today, then, when we are reproached for the wrongs which we commit, and when we ought to feel God's wrath, let us turn to this that is set before us—to the fact that Jesus Christ justly refused to answer. Despite the extreme afflictions which he endured, and the utter severity shown by God toward him, he nevertheless quietly suffered all things, so that by his obedience we should be reconciled to God.

We ourselves are also exhorted to conform to his example. Not that we can perfectly humble ourselves before God, but we should strive to do so. When God, I say, is pleased to chasten us, and when we feel his hand so rough upon us that we fear we will be pressed too hard, we must nevertheless be silent and acknowledge that God is just and fair. Let no complaint be heard from our lips: rather let us glorify God by our very silence, for we are sinners who stand condemned for our misdeeds, and who have nothing to say by way of reply. Peter applies this verse in just this way. When we are afflicted by God's hand, he writes, and even when we are persecuted by the hand of men, we should not cease to endure with patience the wrongs done to us (1 Pet. 2:20). We know that God is seeking to test us, or else is punishing us for our faults. And let us beware of making petty excuses, as many do who plead their weaknesses, their infirmity, their inability to keep silent while God continues to afflict them so severely.

We must try to conform to the Son of God. He is our mirror and our pattern—not, as I said, that we can display equal strength: although we cannot come close to him, this should be our aim. Moreover David was, as we know, a frail man just like us, yet he did not fail to put this teaching into practice. Thus he declares in one place: 'Lord, since it was your hand that lay heavy on me, I said not a word' (cf. Psa. 38:13). And in another place:

'Because my enemies had not been bridled, I suffered their abuse and insults in silence' (cf. Psa. 39:10).

Now because God's Son chose silence in order to give glory to God, and because amid all his sufferings he made no protest or answered back, we must allow God to chasten us as he wills, and to test our obedience by giving the wicked their head so that they persecute us. We cannot, however, make this our aim, unless we are certain of this truth, that when our Lord remained silent before God his Father and before men, it was by this means that he made up for our faults and rebelliousness. In addition, when we read that by his silence he obtained righteousness for us, we see that his silence confers this benefit on us, that by it he upheld our cause and is now our advocate before God. His mouth is always open, being ever ready to intercede in order to remedy all the offences we have committed. It was because he suffered utmost persecution, but made no reply, that he obtained this office, so that, if our consciences condemn us in God's sight, and if, admitting our guilt, we have nothing to say which might excuse us, he will nevertheless defend us, and God will judge us as innocent, because our wrongs have been put right. This must therefore be our starting point. If we begin here, we will be much more motivated, much better disposed to remain silent when afflicted by the hand of God.

Here the prophet adds another thought: *He was taken up from anguish—or from prison* (that is one meaning of the word)—*and from judgment.* Some interpret this to mean that Jesus Christ was suddenly swept off to death as if by force. Rather what Scripture says is that in dying he was not defeated but rose again by the power of God his Father. We are already privileged if we know that our Lord Jesus suffered for our salvation. When we examine our lives it is clear that, without this remedy, we were lost and condemned. Nevertheless, if we were told only about our Lord's death and passion, we would still harbour doubts and misgivings.

How could we hope that he would give us life since death had destroyed him? We would discern no divine or heavenly power which would help us attain steadfast trust in him. We would see only weakness in his death, and we would be dismayed.

So just as the prophet had earlier spoken of the fruit of the death and passion of Jesus Christ, he now adds that he will be taken up by the power of God from distress and judgment. Although he was condemned, God did not abandon him in his hour of need. He raised him high to a position of sovereign power, that he might have dominion over every creature. This is what Paul tells us in the first chapter of Romans, when he writes that he was shown to be the Son of God by his resurrection (Rom. 1:4). If we contemplate our Lord Jesus Christ only in his life, which he lived on earth among men, and again in his death, we will not find in him what is necessary for our salvation. Of course, the miracles he performed, the teaching he proclaimed and the other signs he gave were meant to designate him as the Son of God—supposing, at least, that we were not too weak in faith. Even so we would still remain puzzled and confused, given that Jesus Christ appeared as an ordinary man, a man held moreover in contempt. And finally we would have seen him submitting to an accursed and shameful death. If, however, we pass from his death to his resurrection, this is how we know that our Lord Jesus has won the victory for us.

Paul says the same in a passage in 2 Corinthians: 'He died in the weakness of his flesh but rose by the power of God his Father' (2 Cor. 13:4). Isaiah's argument, then, is meant to remove all doubt that Jesus Christ has the gift of life in his hands, and that he is Lord and Master, for such he is seen to be. Be sure, therefore, that the Son of God became as nothing for our sake, but that at the same time he was not stripped of his power, so that if he kept it hidden for a short time, we have sure proof of it in his resurrection.

Accordingly, we have no excuse for not fixing our trust wholly in him, and for not boldly defying sin and the devil, since Jesus Christ triumphed over them, and since God's hand upheld him and delivered him from all distress. It was then that he exalted him to make him his representative, and to give him, as I said, sovereign rule over the world. This is what we must bear in mind when we read that he was taken up from prison and from judgment.

It was most necessary that our Lord Jesus should descend to the very depths before he was exalted to heavenly glory, for if he had appeared only in his majesty, how could we be assured today that our sins have been forgiven us? We would indeed behold the Son of God who is the source of life, but he would somehow be remote from us; we would have nothing in common with him, nor could we draw near to him. Moreover we would still have cause to despair, since we are guilty of endless offences. And if our Lord Jesus Christ had descended to the very depths without being lifted up to heaven, where would we be? We would still be like poor lifeless souls, always and forever anxious. We would be dreadfully tormented by the thought that God's wrath continually rested on us. When, on the other hand, Scripture says that he was first condemned and suffered awful agony in order to secure our release, and then that, since, as we mentioned yesterday, we have peace with God, we now know that he loves us, is gracious to us and receives us in mercy—when we know that Jesus Christ was taken up, we may conclude that this was done in order to draw us to himself, so that we might share in the glory given to him by God his Father.

Consider what the prophet says next: *Who will tell of his generation?* In saying this Isaiah makes it clear that our Lord's resurrection had full and decisive effect, for all time. It was not some temporary thing which soon ebbs away and vanishes. This is a most important point, for some have taken the word 'generation' to refer to the eternal generation of our Lord Jesus Christ, who was begotten of God his Father from all eternity.[1] Others have turned the prophet's words this way and that, but when we look closely at them all, there is no doubt that the exaltation bestowed on Jesus Christ was not intended for him or his person, nor was it only for a day. No, he has obtained life for us forever, just as Paul says: 'He died to sin once for all, but now he lives to God, and he will never die' (Rom. 6:10). In this way Paul teaches that the sacrifice which our Lord Jesus offered ought truly to satisfy us, for by it he has perfectly sanctified us (Heb. 10:14).

Our Lord, then, did not have to suffer many times. Because he possessed the power to wipe all our sins away once and for all, let us boldly come for refuge to his death and passion, and let us not doubt that they are potent enough to reconcile us to God. The life into which our Lord Jesus Christ has entered is indeed heavenly; the position which he now enjoys is, without question, perfect. When Paul writes that 'he lives to God', he means that Jesus Christ is now free of all misery, free of the mortal condition which he earlier took from us. He threw it off, and is now separated from all human frailties, in order that we who are his members might hope the same for ourselves.

Isaiah, therefore, would have us recognize, first, that our Lord Jesus Christ was raised up, never again to be subject to death; the life he obtained endures forever. Second, we must note that this was done not only for his own sake but for the sake of his whole church. In the same way it is said in the Psalms that God ascended on high and took spoils from his enemies (Psa. 68:18). This was meant to show that when Jesus Christ was exalted after his death, everything served to benefit the church and to work

[1] In his *Commentary* on Isa. 53:8, Calvin attributes this view to certain of the Church Fathers, mentioning Chrysostom by name. Engammare (*SC* IV/1:92) suggests that Münster or Leo Jud, translator of the Zurich Bible, may be meant.

for its common salvation. He defeated sin and Satan in order to free us from them, and to allow us to enjoy the fruit of his victory and to triumph in it. That, in sum, is what this passage teaches us. The main thing, however, is to put it into practice!

So when we read that he was taken up from anguish and condemnation, we should learn, when we are tempted somehow to despair, to set Jesus Christ before our eyes, remembering that he passed this way. Remember too that God his Father put forth his hand so that he was not crushed, and that he did it for our sake. There is thus a way by which we may escape distress, for we have Jesus Christ as our commander; we can follow in his steps, because everything that was done in him, as in our Head, is ours; its outcome will be seen in each and every believer.

When we read also of his generation, we are meant to see that he will have the power to sustain his church to the very end, for he has no wish to be separated from his body. It is true that his position is very different from ours, until we are taken out of this world. Even so he is always the first-born from the dead, and the first of those destined to rise (1 Cor. 15:20; Col. 1:18). Bear in mind, then, that because God's Son is immortal, not only in his being and divine majesty but in his flesh and human nature, it is so that the church should always be protected in this world and should never perish. If we rely firmly on this verse, we should be absolutely sure of the church's permanence. Admittedly we will see great disturbances which appear to show that God's church must perish. It only takes a storm to arise and to whip up great and dreadful waves, for us to cry: 'We are finished! All is lost!' We know this from experience. How likely is it that God's church will continue, seeing that it is attacked from all sides? Suffering so many assaults, does it not seem destined to be utterly destroyed?

Whatever the case, we must come to him who is its Head. And since the generation of our Lord Jesus Christ does not end and undergoes no change so that nothing stops him remembering to protect his church, let us be confident, even though there be trials greater and more severe than any today. This is something which applies not only to the whole fellowship of the faithful but also to each one of us. So may we both know and be persuaded that although our life is but a breath, and although we should be prepared to vanish from one minute to the next, the life we have is permanent, since we are members of our Lord Jesus Christ. At the same time let us learn to pass through this world, for the life we presently enjoy is not our real life: it is a passage through which we must quickly run until we reach the rest which is part of our inheritance. Therefore, since we hope for eternal life, we ought to leave all this behind; it is nothing but a shadow. Our minds should not be engrossed by all that is visible to us, and which might make us want to remain in this world, for most surely those who settle only for the world separate themselves from God's Son, and do not deserve to have part and portion of eternity with him. Let us withdraw, then, from this world, if we would be united with the Son of God.

In addition, the prophet seeks to give greater force and vigour to his message by suddenly intervening to exclaim, like a man amazed: 'Who will tell of his generation?' This is a warning to us to fight hard against all trials, so that, if we meet hindrances here and there, if, as well as being troubled, we are more or less overwhelmed, we should nevertheless resist and strive with all our might until we attain that to which Isaiah points—the fact, that is, that the human mind cannot comprehend the generation of our Lord, and cannot express it in words. We must thus rise above all our thoughts if we are to trust in our Lord Jesus Christ and to follow him, so that we may share in the eternal inheritance he has obtained for us. It is not a matter of fixing on some belief or idea which might explain this truth, as if it could be argued over in words alone. Remember that while our faith depends on hearing, it will never have assurance until it receives testimony from God and from his Holy Spirit, a testimony which transcends anything that human language might express. That is why our own perceptions must never hold us back and lead us to judge as we think fit. We must understand that it is a wonderful mystery, beyond our understanding, that the only Son of God became a mortal man, and was subject to death in order to secure our release; and that now, amid our frailties, we nevertheless have life which is permanent, which we possess by faith until it is revealed at the last day, and at his coming. That is what this verse tells us.

Once more the prophet adds: *He was cut off from the land of the living, and suffered wounds which were owed to his people.* This verse confirms what was said a little while ago: our Lord's generation was not only for himself, but for the whole body of the church to which he is united, and to which he is inseparably bound. Were it not so, the prophet teaches that the death and passion of our Lord Jesus Christ would serve no purpose. Now it is an intolerable blasphemy to think that God's Son came down into the world and endured a cruel death, that God's judgment fell upon his head, that he was punished for our sins and was held to be the greatest evildoer on earth, yet that it all conferred no benefit on believers! We might think the whole thing was a joke!

Thus the prophet calls us to consider why and to what end our Lord Jesus was smitten and stricken. As we said before, it was no accident. And we must not only think of the hands of men and of those who unjustly put him to death; we must look up with the eyes of faith to the counsel of God, by which he determined that Jesus Christ should be sacrificed, in order to obtain forgiveness of sins for us. We are therefore led to conclude that Jesus Christ did not suffer for his own sake, but that he suffered the wounds which were owed to us. So the first thing we are urged to do, whenever our Lord's death and passion are laid before us, is to acknowledge our sins and to examine them. God of course displays the treasures of his goodness. That is why Paul, having first outlined how we are justified by faith, and how we may boldly come before God and boast that we will be acceptable to him; and having further declared that God will not reject us poor sinners but will uphold us, since he welcomes us for the sake of his only Son—Paul, I say, goes on to appeal to the brethren 'by the goodness and mercies of God' (Rom. 12:1). He thus makes it clear that in Jesus Christ's suffering we have proof of God's boundless love. It is as if God were revealing to us his very heart, his innermost self, in order to testify how dear we are to him, and how precious our souls are to him.

Naturally this should not cause us to slumber so that we each revel in our sins. The more generous God has been to us in the person of our Lord Jesus Christ, the more unthinkable it should be for us to feel hostility toward him, to war with his righteousness and to earn his displeasure. No, the grace God has shown to us in Jesus Christ ought always to draw us to repentance.

Today the papists try falsely to malign the truth we preach, namely that we must be saved by God's unmerited goodness and that we must turn to Jesus Christ for refuge, knowing that it is in him that we have full and perfect righteousness. 'Ah yes,' they cry, 'so everyone is bound to live as they please, and to have no scruples about offending God!' Now these dogs can only bark like this because they have no idea what it is to have one's sins forgiven. These pious frauds utterly mock God and all religion; they have never perceived what it means to have transgressed God's law. We know too how they try to clear themselves. If they have sung mass, mumbled prayers, performed a few tricks and other such piffling nonsense, God ought to be appeased, like a child with a small rattle. This is the way these despisers of God blaspheme against the gospel. When we, on the other hand, know our sins and the reason why God's priceless grace is preached to us, we are sure to be drawn to repentance and to be mortally pierced with horror and anguish. We are conscious that God is against us, for we have provoked his wrath. This is Isaiah's message to us here: Jesus Christ suffered the wounds which were owed to us.

In saying this, the prophet is pointing out that we can never have a lively sense of what we have gained from our Lord's death and passion, unless we feel deep down how much we have offended God and have made him our judge and our enemy—until, that is, we are reconciled to him through his unmerited goodness. This is something very often taught to us in Scripture. The main thing, however, is that we strive hard to put this teaching into practice.

At any rate, we see that our Lord Jesus Christ calls only those who labour and are heavy laden (Matt. 11:28). Accordingly, he excludes all who slumber in their iniquities, who are at ease in them or who throw caution to the winds, having no fear of God. Those who freely indulge in evil cannot draw near to Jesus Christ. That is quite certain. What, after all, can give us access to him, except his own words of invitation? The same is true of those who are blinded by their pride and arrogance, and who pretend that they are righteous in themselves. To these also the door is most certainly closed: they can hope for no relief from our Lord Jesus Christ. Why not? 'Come to me,' he says. What? Everybody? True, he does call everyone, but he makes a distinction: 'You who labour and are heavy laden.' So having called to all who need his help, he shows that none can benefit unless they labour and are heavy laden. When, therefore, we feel our burdens and groan beneath them, when we know that we are absolutely exhausted, that is when the path by which we can come to Jesus Christ is open to us, for his arms are outstretched to receive us. As we will later see, he was sent to preach to those who were downcast in spirit. In the same way we must be made a sacrifice, so that we conform to the pattern of our Lord.

It is true that the sacrifice which he offered is our only hope: we must not presume to contribute anything of our own. Jesus Christ obtained full salvation for us when he offered himself as a sacrifice to God his Father. Even so we need the threat of God's judgment; we need to recognize how dire it is for us, miserable earthworms, to rise up against the majesty of him who created us, and to transgress his law. We are in this world to serve and honour him. Let us feel these things keenly, then, within ourselves, so that we may come to our Lord Jesus Christ.

We might at first glance think it odd that the prophet should add by way of explanation: 'He was cut off from the land of the living.' Because our Lord Jesus Christ was exalted and because he now rules in heaven and on earth, it seems inappropriate that the means first chosen was that he should be cut off, for before the world was made he always possessed the glory in which he now is, as he affirms in the seventeenth chapter of John (John 17:5) As to his divine being, he acquired nothing new. To be destroyed, as it were, by death, is not the path by which heavenly glory is attained; to be condemned by a mortal man is not designed to make him judge of the world! The fact is that God chose to work in a way which is beyond human understanding. Nor ought we to offer our opinion, as if we were in a position to criticize God's counsel, which we know to be the cause and origin of our salvation. In all humility we should glorify God for allowing his Son to be cut off from the land of the living.

Now Isaiah speaks explicitly of Jesus Christ as if he had been completely crushed; he describes not an ordinary death, but one intended to annihilate him, as if the very memory of him had been entirely blotted out. For although every person must die, and thus be cut off from the land of the living, what was exceptional about our Lord Jesus Christ was that his death served to exclude him from the ranks of men. It was, as we have said, a shameful death, one cursed by God. There was, at the same time, the pit of hell. Not that it swallowed him up; he did, however, struggle against the pangs of death. The prophet is therefore right to portray him as one who was banished from human society.[2]

Whatever the case, by this means and in the very nature that he took from us, he attained such majesty that now, while being our brother, he is also our judge. This is how Paul describes him when he says that he was obedient to death—a truly accursed death (Phil. 2:8). In speaking of his obedience Paul stresses what we already noticed in Isaiah, that everything our Lord endured was done voluntarily. And because we are guilty before God and are therefore his enemies, Scripture says that he yielded. He who had all dominion and authority took the form of a servant, and assumed the condition of those who, as Paul writes, were under the yoke (Gal. 5:1). He was thus obedient throughout his life, choosing to live under the law. That was not all, for although he had a fearful expectation of death, to the point that, sweating water and blood, he pleaded: 'Father, if it be possible, let this bitter drink be taken from me', he nevertheless pulled back, saying: 'Your will, not mine, be done' (Matt. 26:39; Mark 14:36; Luke 22:42). Thereupon Paul adds that this was why God exalted him and gave him a name which is above all names, so that every knee should bow before him (Phil. 2:9-10).

Know, then, that even in our human nature Jesus Christ possesses supreme majesty; so we may come to him in full confidence. For on what grounds is he now the judge of all the

[2] It is thus that Calvin interprets Christ's descent into hell, as affirmed by the Apostles' Creed. Cf. *Inst.* II.16.10: 'Nothing could have been achieved if Jesus Christ had simply endured bodily death. It was necessary for him to bear in his soul the severity of the vengeance of God his Father, to confront his wrath and to satisfy his judgment. Hence he was required to struggle against the forces of hell, and to fight hand to hand against the dread of everlasting death ... It is no surprise if he is said to have descended into hell, for he suffered that same death by which God in his wrath punishes evildoers.'

world? It is because he not only became a brother to us but offered himself as surety for us and bore all our iniquities. He was smitten and stricken by the hand of God that we might be protected from the wounds which we had merited. That is why he is now exalted, and why we are able to draw near to him with boldness. Evildoers, it is true, and devils, despite themselves, are bound to feel that the Son of God stands over them, for all his enemies must be trodden beneath his feet (Psa. 110:1). We, for our part, must willingly do him homage, quietly submit to him and recognize the majesty which is his in his human nature, so that we have cause to boast in triumph over sin.

That Isaiah's prophecy refers to Jesus Christ is clear from Luke's account of the eunuch who had come to Jerusalem to worship in the temple (Acts 8:27-39). He was reading this passage which was explained to him by Philip, who, transported by the angel, had been sent by God for the purpose of coming to this man who was seeking God. Like a poor blind soul, however, he as yet possessed no knowledge. Philip explained the passage, with the result that by this one proclamation the eunuch was converted to our Lord Jesus Christ and asked to be baptized in his name.

This story should touch us deeply, for to begin with it teaches us that if at first we cannot purely comprehend the message of our Lord Jesus Christ, and the fruit which we should derive from what is daily preached to us, this is no reason to despair. We must keep searching Scripture for the things we do not know. God will hold out his hand to us; he will have mercy on us and will direct us to the proper goal.

Now since this poor man, who was busy reading Scripture but who failed to grasp its meaning, was converted to Jesus Christ, let us be careful that we do not go to sleep. Let us rather follow what is said in the Psalm: 'Today, if you hear his voice, do not harden your hearts' (Psa. 95:8). We should so relish the teaching which is here proclaimed that we, being led to our Lord Jesus Christ, may accept him and cling to him with genuine, steadfast faith. Let us seek to profit, and may we be ever strengthened in our faith. And having truly humbled ourselves, let us come before our God to ask forgiveness. Despite our unworthiness we should not fail to hold our heads high, and to attain true assurance that God will receive us for the sake of our great Redeemer. Although he was overwhelmed for a short time, let us keep in view the fact that he was raised above the heavens, in order to draw us to himself, as he says in the twelfth chapter of John: 'When I am lifted up from the earth, I will draw all men to myself' (John 12:32).

Now let us cast ourselves down before the majesty of our good God, acknowledging our faults and praying that he may make us feel them more than in the past. May he be pleased to open our eyes and to touch our hearts, so that we may submit more completely to his will, using the means which he shows us in his word. May we, that is, hate and abhor all our sins, so that we may be open to receiving the grace which he has revealed to us, once and for all, in our Lord Jesus Christ, and which he desires us now to enjoy in and through the gospel.

5

SEED FOR MANY GENERATIONS

He laid open his grave to the wicked and his death to the rich, even though he had committed no offence, nor was any deceit found in his mouth. 10 *Nevertheless the Lord chose to afflict him with infirmity, and when he has made his soul a satisfaction for sin, he will see his seed of many generations, and God's pleasure will prosper in his hand* (Isa. 53:9-10).

THE prophet continues the same message here as we noted before, which was that there was such enmity between God and us that the only way to appease his wrath was for Jesus Christ to answer, utterly and completely, for us. We may gather from the supreme suffering endured by the Son of God how dire our offences are, and how abhorrent they are to God, for as we have heard, and as we will soon hear again, there was nothing unnecessary or superfluous about the death and passion of our Lord Jesus Christ. Because he was grievously afflicted, on the one hand he has testified to his boundless goodness to us and to the love he bore us. On the other hand, we must reflect on all that our sins deserved in the sight of God.

Now here we are told that, in addition to what we have already read, our Lord Jesus Christ was exposed to the constant mockery and abuse of the wicked, in which they gloried. For by the word *grave* Isaiah undoubtedly means that Jesus Christ was subject to every kind of insult, and that, in a sense, God had determined to forsake him for a time, leaving men free to revile him, as we see from what the gospel narrative tells us. Not only was Jesus Christ crucified, but everyone put out their tongue at him, threw taunts at him and even tried to drive him to despair, if that were possible. This accorded with what was said in Psalm 22, that the foulest and most rascally would put out their tongues at him (Psa. 22:7). We hear too their cries: 'He saved others, let him save himself if he can! Why does he not call upon God? We will see if God really loves him!' (Matt. 27:42-43).

That is how our Lord Jesus was savaged by the wicked, and there was no limit to the fury which people felt for him. All this, so that we might obtain such grace before God that all the blame which we deserved was hidden. All this, so that however much Satan, with good reason, might accuse us, those things we are ashamed of might be buried. Thus our Lord Jesus chose to endure men's insults and accusations, in order that, in God's sight, all our vileness might be covered and never again remembered.

In speaking of *the rich*, the prophet is referring in effect to the most violent of men, to those who freely indulge in abuse of every kind. We know that when people are respected and have plenty of this world's goods, they inspire fear and even dread; they always misuse their power. We will find very few who are self-controlled and even-tempered, and who are kind when they have the means of doing ill. The poor, by contrast, are very proud within themselves, but are restrained by necessity, so no one sees the evil in them; it remains hidden. The rich, however, and those who are well off, are ungovernable; they think that everything is allowed them. In short, the prophet here reveals that Jesus Christ was placed, so to speak, into men's hands, and was so evilly treated that in the eyes of all he ranked below the most despicable of men. He was like an earthworm (Psa. 22:6) and was the target of everyone's mockery. That is the thrust of this first clause.

At the same time Isaiah adds that *he had nevertheless done no wrong*, showing that God's Son, being entirely innocent, willingly took upon himself all our burdens which would have overwhelmed us. No mortal being exists who could sustain all that our Lord Jesus bore and suffered. So once again the prophet insists that it was not for his demerits or any guilt in him that people were so hostile and cruel to him, and behaved in so tyrannical a way toward him. It was all because of us, because if we consider how Jesus Christ lived, we find that no one had any grounds for laying violent hands on him. True, the priests told Pilate that if he had not been an offender, they would not have brought him before him (John 18:30). The fact is that if we ask what wrongs he had done, he did good to everyone! He gave light to the blind, caused the lame to walk, and fed the people when they were hungry. In a word, all the riches of God's goodness and mercy are seen displayed in him.

Why then was he so cruelly persecuted? There has to be some other cause, which is why the prophet, when speaking of our Lord's blamelessness, brings us back to our sins and offences. We must not think that Isaiah's aim here is simply to justify the Son of God. It would be too slight a thing to say: 'Look, he was guilty of nothing, but behaved in such a way that all should love and honour him.' That is very true, but it would be much too cold to teach that Jesus Christ deserved to be excused or to be cleared of all blame. No, the prophet sought to look higher up, and to combine the two points which he makes here: that God exposed his only Son to insults and abuse of every kind, and that he was nevertheless innocent.

If people had risen up against him, but if this had happened apart from the providence and counsel of God, we might say that it was their fury which drove them to it, but that would not have been the cause. Scripture says that it was the hand of God. Although the priests, all the Jews in general and the soldiers had been led by the devil to spew forth blasphemies against our Lord, as the gospel tells us, they would not have done it, declares Isaiah, if God had not ordained it. We should not fix our eyes solely on men, so that we say, 'They did this, and they did that.' It was God's verdict, just as surely as if he had been seated above on his judgment throne and had delivered his only Son into the hands of tyrants and evildoers, allowing all kinds of insults to be heaped upon him, yet with no blame attaching to him. We therefore read that not only did men not spare our Lord Jesus Christ, neither did God his Father. As John says, 'God so loved the world that he revealed it in the person of his Son, by giving him up to so bitter a death for us' (cf. John 3:16). If, then, we look up, and recognize that nothing was done to our Lord Jesus Christ which was not determined by God himself, we will conclude that if Jesus Christ was blameless—as he was!—it was there that our sins were visibly on show, and that all the reproaches and insults directed against him should have come instead to us.

We should therefore understand that we deserve to see every creature arming itself to demand vengeance against us, and although they have neither tongue nor mouth, they are witness to our shame and offences. We are undone in the sight of both heaven and earth.

This is the first point for us to notice. Either God brought such torment upon his Son on a mere whim, or else he had to demonstrate how awful our sins were, and how much we deserved to be reviled on every hand. Admittedly we are incapable of showing tolerance to the slightest degree: we are so sensitive that if people touch our honour, our instinct is to rail against them. This is because we do not think about what we are really like or consider whether we are being rightly or wrongly criticized. Be sure, then, that although the reproaches we deserve have been blotted out by our Lord Jesus Christ, we need to be brought to repentance by God. When we do not voluntarily examine ourselves and feel ashamed, God raises up men who will wake us up. The more we attempt to shelter behind empty excuses, the more he uncovers our shameful ways and makes them known.

Among the fruits of repentance, Paul says that in thinking about our past life, we should hang our heads and groan before God, feeling ashamed of ourselves (2 Cor. 7:11). Yet who does this as perfectly as he should? Instead, we try hypocritically to forget about our faults. God, however, wants us to recall them and to take account of them, since we seek to conceal them by underhand means.

Remember nevertheless that we are now able to come before God and his angels with the assurance that our failings will not be on display, and that our vileness will not be disclosed, since our Lord Jesus Christ has borne our reproach. This was no accident, nor did men take anything from him which was not in accord with God's will. God planned it that way; it was a determination made in heaven. Because our Lord Jesus was righteous, it was necessary that he should take our burdens on himself, and thus suffer affliction.

Know, then, that we deserve to be disgraced, and yet we are absolved because Jesus Christ has cleared us and has made satisfaction for us. That is why Isaiah speaks here of the Son of God's innocence and integrity, not in order to justify him but to make us feel exactly who we are, and where we were heading if we had not been rescued and redeemed. For the rest, the prophet, intending to show how consummate was our Lord's work, how much beyond reproach, adds that *there was no deceit found in his mouth.*

Now according to James, someone would need to be perfect indeed if no vile word ever escaped his lips, given that the tongue is the frailest thing there is (James 3:2). And although we are much too prone to evil, he who can restrain his hands and feet and can lead so disciplined a life as to display only godliness and virtue, cannot control his tongue so well without some flippant, thoughtless, false or insincere word making its appearance. In short, we are told that in our Lord Jesus Christ no deceit was found, proving that he was a mirror of holiness in all that he said and did. There can be no doubt that all the ills we suffer are the fruit of our sins, for if we had remained in the innocence in which God had placed our father Adam, there would be nothing in the world for which we might be reproached. All would be wiped away. The fact that we are reproached is the fruit of our sins. We therefore conclude that because no blemish—no, not the slightest—was found in Jesus Christ, he bore the punishment which we deserved.

Next, the prophet adds this comment: *God chose to afflict him with infirmity.* The word 'infirmity' has a very broad meaning in Scripture. It includes everything which might bring someone into contempt, as can be seen from a number of passages. If we are wretched, weak in body or held up to scorn, if someone is coarse in looks, speech or action, disagreeable in behaviour or lacking in dexterity, Scripture describes him as infirm. Here Isaiah returns to an earlier theme, that in appearance our Lord was marred, and that people saw no reason why he should be in any way esteemed among men. Not, however, that he was without certain marks which made him worthy of honour as God's only Son, but these were veiled by his suffering and by men's perception of him as weak, so weak indeed that he seemed devoid of any quality which people might admire. We should remember also what we said before, that he was smitten and stricken by God's hand, that he endured the dreadful anguish of his judgment and bore in his body the most frightful torture imaginable. And besides all that, he was reviled as if he was not worthy to be ranked among the lowest villains. That was how the Son of God was afflicted.

Observe, therefore, that it was because God did not spare him that we ourselves are spared. Even so he has given us cause to humble ourselves, so that we no longer come with heads held high, trying to justify ourselves and seeking to cast our sins behind our backs. Daily we should remember them with shame, as we see the ransom which was paid for them. Was it so small a thing? Supposing we heard of some wretched offender who had committed a host of thefts and robberies, and who acknowledged his crimes. Now if, instead, the son of some king was brought to trial and made to suffer punishment, while the offender was acquitted and fully cleared, would he be likely to mock and jeer when he saw that the king's son was to pay his penalty and die for him?

Now we are the ones who have been spared. Here we see Jesus Christ, God's only Son, who is imprisoned while we are freed; he is condemned while we are absolved; he was exposed to every form of shame, while our honour is secure; he went down to the pit of hell, while an opening has been made for us to enter the kingdom of heaven. When we hear of all these things, is this the time to stay asleep, to take our ease and to complacently accept our sins? Let us attend, then, to the Holy Spirit's meaning, and carefully weigh the statement that it was God who chose to afflict him. We are not to think that our Lord was left entirely by himself, and that the wicked were able to torment him as they pleased. They could do nothing apart from God's counsel, as Peter says in Acts: 'God did the things his hand and counsel had determined' (Acts 2:23; 4:28).

Isaiah rightly points us to the fact that we must lift our minds to God, knowing that, because he is judge of the world, he has accepted satisfaction for our sins and offences from his only Son, so that we might be acquitted. Not without purpose, then, was Jesus Christ brutally smitten. This was so that we might walk with heads held high, conscious that God chose not to remember our evil ways which made us abhorrent to him. To know this is to have gained a great deal, not only for a day but for the whole of our life. In truth, this is teaching to which we must attend, for however well we think we know it, we should strive more and more to live by it.

The prophet expresses this thought more fully in what follows: *He will lay down his soul to make satisfaction for sin.* In other words, Jesus Christ will disregard his life in order to secure redemption for us, as a price for our sins and iniquities. Here again, the prophet sets before us the Son of God's willing obedience, for having said on the one hand that the Father chose to afflict him, Isaiah now declares that the Son, for his part, voluntarily accepted it all. He was not coerced, but came forward of his own accord to be the true sacrificial offering.

Now it was always the custom for men to offer sacrifice to God with, as we say, free and reverent hearts. By the same token, it was necessary for our Lord Jesus to offer himself and to submit to the death that he endured. Were it not for that, as we said yesterday, no remedy would have been found for our rebelliousness in God's sight; but since he laid down his soul, since, that is, he was ready and prepared to suffer the condemnation which was owed to us, we may now have, by his death, full assurance of salvation. As he himself said in John's Gospel, 'No one will take my life from me; I will lay it down of my own free will' (John 10:18). It is true that his life was taken from him when he was crucified, and we know what cruelty and fury drove those who crucified him. Nevertheless they could do nothing against him, supposing that this was what they wanted and had striven for, if this had not been done according to the ordinance and decree of God the Father, just as we saw in the passage from Acts. In addition, however, and at the same time, our Lord Jesus Christ freely consented to the verdict which, for our sake, was brought against him. It is in this way that he laid down his life.

He laid it down, says the prophet, on account of our sin. The word 'sin' is used in connection with all types of sacrifice, because anyone who had done wrong and who sought pardon, came bearing a sacrifice, laying his sin upon it. It is as if he were saying, 'Alas, O God, I am guilty of death in your sight. I am an offender. I could not bear the punishment which I owe; it would be a burden which would completely crush me. Yet here is the remedy. I am asking you for pardon by means of the sacrifice which I have offered to you.' This was why such sacrifices were called 'sin offerings', because the curse which we deserved and which would have destroyed us, was, as it were, laid upon the head of a calf, a sheep or on anything else which was offered (Lev. 4:13-33).

All this was a symbolic rite under the law. Hence our Lord Jesus Christ is called a sin offering, for he suffered our curse so that we might be blessed by God his Father. Do not think that this detracts from his majesty. Instead, he deserves all the more praise from us, as Paul points out in his second letter to the Corinthians, when he writes that 'he who knew no sin was made sin for us, that we might become the righteousness of God in him' (2 Cor. 5:21). Without question, Paul intends to show us the fruit of our Lord's death and passion, just as Isaiah had done. Jesus Christ was innocent and without blemish, which is why it was his task to bear the burden of others. He bore it in such a way that he was made sin; he took our curse upon himself. To what end? To answer for us so that, in God's sight, we might be righteous. The obedience of our Lord Jesus Christ is like a cloak which covers all our transgressions. His blood, too, is for our cleansing, when we are bathed in it and are sprinkled with it by the Holy Spirit, as Peter says (1 Pet. 1:2).

This, then, is the essence of what we are told. To repeat what I have said, if we are to hate our wrongs and feel disgust at ourselves, we must think of what the Son of God endured. We should thrill with wonder at such a thing, that he who is the fount of all righteousness was made sin, and that he who is blessed and who sanctifies all things—yes, even the angels in heaven—was made a curse. When these things are said, we find them difficult and strange, but we do not have the wit or wisdom to use them for our instruction. Since the Son of God went to this extreme, could we possibly find a remedy anywhere else? Absolutely not! We can readily judge that neither men nor angels nor anything else is in a position to help us: we must turn to the Son of God for refuge.

Therefore that devil Servetus, who was executed here, is even more accursed because he falsified and corrupted the Bible by maintaining that this prophecy was about Cyrus, a heathen and idolater. He thus robbed our Lord Jesus Christ of what is properly his. When Isaiah added these details as in a picture of our Lord's crucifixion, things could not have been clearer or more transparent. Nevertheless, this devil went to such deplorable lengths as to rob Jesus Christ of the dignity of his office, claiming that a pagan had suffered for the people, when out of ambition and greed he went to war, seeking to spill human blood. He thereby reaped his reward.[1]

Now this is a terrible perversion of so fine a prophecy. No living creature ever imagined the meaning which this poor

[1] It was doubtless the death of Cyrus in battle (530 BC) which explains the suffering motif. Generally speaking, it is rare for Calvin to cite a critic by name. The Spanish savant Michael Servetus (1511–53), notorious for his radical views on the Trinity, was sought by authorities on both sides of the confessional divide. Imprisoned in France on the charge of heresy, he escaped but was arrested four months later in Geneva, tried, and executed in October 1553. Almost six years after the event, the memory was still fresh in Calvin's mind. Further critical references to Servetus will be found in sermons on 1 Timothy (*CO* 53:324; see also Calvin, *Sermons on 1 Timothy*, tr. Robert White [Edinburgh: Banner of Truth, 2019], pp. 410-11) and Titus (*CO* 54:547; see also Calvin, *Sermons on Titus*, tr. Robert White [Edinburgh: Banner of Truth, 2015], pp. 47, 216).

wretch dreamed up, for although there have been many heretics who have recklessly corrupted the teaching of holy Scripture, they have never gone to those lengths. All the marks of reprobation were bound to appear in that unhappy man.

So when the prophet refers to our Lord Jesus Christ, it is, first, to make us feel ashamed, and then to encourage us to praise the priceless goodness of our God, who chose to make his only Son sin for our sake. Nor did our Lord himself refuse but, forgetting himself as it were, he willingly descended to the most terrible of depths, in order to bear our curse in its entirety. Remember, then, that we have no other means of clearing ourselves before God, unless first place is given to the atoning sacrifice which he offered once and for all.

Admittedly, the world always attempts to recompense God by devising one means or another. As we said earlier, we see many examples of this among the papists, who try to appease God with any amount of tomfoolery. They insist that we cannot be absolved without satisfactions, for although God in his unmerited kindness forgives our guilt, punishment is nevertheless retained until each of us is finally cleared. It is on this that purgatory is based. We cannot, they say, make satisfaction in this life, for there is always a residue, a deficit owing. We must suffer the penalty outside of this world; it is a payment made to God.

Such are the lies and illusions with which the devil has led poor folk astray. It is even more important, then, that we attend to this teaching. Remember that God's law does not say, 'You will serve me in any way or fashion that you choose.' There were sacrifices which the law specified, and ceremonies which it ordained. No one was to go beyond them, and no new forms of worship or other means of obtaining grace were to be devised. Today we must be content with the death and passion of our Lord Jesus Christ, knowing that this is the only means by which God will be propitious and favourable to us, and through which he will accept and adopt us. That is the prophet's meaning here.

What is said next is this: *He will prolong his days, and he will see a generation that lasts forever.* Once more Isaiah recalls us to the glory of our Lord Jesus Christ, in order to give us greater assurance that we can come to him. If he had remained in death, defeated as it were, we could not be justified or quickened by his grace. How could death itself bring righteousness if it was a solitary event? How could it bring life? It is because, along with his sacrificial death, there is resurrection, that we have complete assurance. We now see how victory over sin has been won for us, allowing us to be accounted righteous; and death has been abolished in us so that life might prevail.

In the first place this applies of course to the Son of God himself. As we said before, he died in the weakness of his flesh, but the heavenly power of his Holy Spirit is seen in his resurrection (2 Cor. 13:4). This he demonstrated when he said, 'Destroy this temple, and I will rebuild it on the third day' (John 2:19). In this way, then, our Lord Jesus Christ saw his days prolonged. In rising he did not show himself to men for only a short time, and then to die again. No, having appeared to his disciples, and having appointed them as witnesses to his resurrection, he ascended to heaven, free of the frailty of our human lot. As a result, we can now place our confidence in him, seeing that he has full lordship over death. He has vanquished the devil and has triumphed over him, for having made himself a sacrificial offering, he has been received and exalted to a position of power and dominion, as we explained earlier.

We should note, however, that all of this applies also to the entire body of the church, for Jesus Christ wills not to be separated from it. He says, indeed, that *he will have his seed.* It is true that we are called brethren of Jesus Christ (Heb. 2:11). On no other grounds can we be children of God. He who is the beloved and the only-begotten must accept us, and so unite himself with us that we might have by adoption what is his by nature alone. This does not stop us, however, from being children born of his seed. What, after all, is the true seed of the church? It is indeed the word of the gospel, as Peter writes (1 Pet. 1:23). Here is verified for us what we already saw in the fortieth chapter: God's word endures forever (Isa. 40:8). By it we are made incorruptible provided God's word benefits us, according as the Holy Spirit grants this to us.

Such is the seed by which we are born again to eternal life, as long, that is, as we come to our Lord Jesus Christ. How does the gospel work, and by what power is it able to make us children of God? It is through the blood of Jesus Christ, which is the true, life-giving seed. Isaiah is therefore right to say that he will see his seed for many generations. Once again, we conclude that the blessing which our Lord obtained by his rising again was not intended only for him: it was to give us all a share, and to call us into partnership with him, for we are members of his body.

At the same time, we are warned not to look for a single drop of life in ourselves but to receive it all from our Lord Jesus Christ. How then will God recognize us as his children? How will we have a place in the church? How will we be reckoned among his flock? We must keep coming back to this, that God only accepts us because we have fellowship with Jesus Christ. There is our birth, there is our beginning. Let men boast as much as they like about their free will, which they think prepares them to receive the grace of God. For how can anyone make anything of himself if he has not yet been born from his mother's womb? So bear in mind that it is when we are begotten in Jesus Christ that we have our beginning, our first creation. We can do nothing, and nothing can come from our own efforts. All that we have comes from God's free goodness which is bestowed on us in Jesus Christ.

To help us savour his death and passion all the more, the prophet declares that he will see his seed, *because he has made his soul an offering for sin*. If we fail to exalt God's goodness in the death and passion of our Lord Jesus Christ, we show that our real wish is to wipe out all hope of salvation. All indeed who, in their pride, will not settle for Jesus Christ because he was crucified, are ignorant of the end God had in view. Without it, what would become of us? There would be no church in the world, no salvation—in short, no hope of anything good. If Jesus Christ had not laid down his life and thereby purchased us, we would be ruined, irremediably lost and damned. This is why Scripture so often stresses that we have been bought at so great a price (1 Cor. 6:20; 1 Pet. 1:18-19). Here is a lesson we must remember.

Our text concludes by saying that *the pleasure of God will prosper in his hand*. The word 'pleasure' suggests a beneficent will and unmerited favour, for it would not be enough for our Lord Jesus to carry out God's will: it must be a loving will which bears witness to his fatherly affection. Moses certainly fulfilled God's will by publishing the law, yet see how the thunder and lightning terrified all who were there! There was nothing but the threat of death (Exod. 19:16; Heb. 12:18). Why was this? Because the law could only bring wrath. Men were meant to feel a sense of awful condemnation, and to be filled with terror. There is, however, in God another will which he has revealed in Jesus Christ. In it he has chosen to show mercy by receiving us to himself, by blotting out our sins and by delivering us from our state of condemnation. That is the proper sense of what Isaiah means when he says that God's pleasure will prosper.

He speaks of God's will prospering in his hand, signifying that Jesus Christ is to be the minister and dispenser of God's grace for our salvation. It is true that God could have rescued us from death by another means, but that was not what he willed, nor was it right.[2] He thus appointed our Lord Jesus Christ as the one by whom we might be redeemed and reconciled—by whom, in short, we might obtain what was necessary for our salvation.

Let us sum up, then, all that can be gathered from this verse. 'God's good pleasure,' it says, 'and his unmerited favour will prosper in the hand of Jesus Christ.' Why does the prophet speak this way? It is because we are inclined to be distrustful, and because we meet many hindrances which cause us to lose heart. The Holy Spirit therefore forestalls us, insisting that, whatever happens, God's grace will prove effective and will fulfil its purpose. Whatever the devil does to make sure that our Lord's death and passion are of no avail to us, and produce no fruit in us, and however much we ourselves are so wicked that we wilfully turn away and treat them as pointless, God in his infinite goodness will nevertheless prevail.

In brief, the prophet's purpose in this verse is to declare that not only was the death and passion of our Lord Jesus Christ sufficient for the salvation of the world, but that God will give full effect to them. We will see their fruit, which we will feel and actually experience. From this we gather that the church will always exist in the world, and that whatever the devil contrives and however hard he toils to overthrow what God has built, Jesus Christ will win. The grace which he both ministers and dispenses will prosper and be fulfilled among men. That, after all, is the message of Psalm 2: 'Why have the kings of the earth risen up? Why have they plotted with the people? God in the end will achieve his ends. Yes, they make many plans, but he who

[2] French: *et n'estoit pas bon aussi*. 'Not right', presumably because only the cross could reveal the sinfulness of sin and God's uncompromising justice; and only by the death of his Son could the depth of God's love and the freeness of his grace be made clear to sinners. For Calvin, God is free to act in any way which is consistent with his nature. No external necessity is imposed on him. He might have saved us by a simple word, but chose instead the way of atonement as being most in accord with our needs and his glory (*Inst.* II.12.1-3). See Paul Helm's discussion in *Calvin at the Centre* (Oxford: Oxford University Press, 2010), pp. 163-81.

dwells in heaven laughs at them, until in his wrath he lays bare his arm' (Psa. 2:1-5).

Notice here how the Holy Spirit assures us that our Lord's death and passion remain effective and enable the church to endure, so that it is never undone by the attacks, storms and whirlwinds which its enemies and their leader, Satan, might stir up. Moreover, the word 'prosper' is used to show that God will cause the death and passion of Jesus Christ to flourish and to bear more and more fruit. And just when this work seems close to destruction, God will raise it up again and will overcome whatever might stop it reaching its goal.

For the rest, we should all take care to apply this teaching to ourselves, never doubting that although our wings hang limp and although sin still holds us captive, God will deliver us from our captivity and will accomplish the work begun in us, making up for what we now lack (Phil. 1:6). How is this done? By coming to Jesus Christ. He will set to work, for that is the task committed to him; that is the office which he has received from God his Father.

Let us therefore be content to know that, having been ordained minister of our salvation, he will achieve it without fail, for this has been determined. Let us also make good use of the verse we cited earlier (1 Cor. 6:20), so that, by hearing the message which is daily brought to us, we might share in the fruit of our Lord's death and passion. It is not enough that Jesus Christ should himself have suffered, being made a sacrifice for us. We must be assured of this through the gospel, whose testimony we should accept. Let us not doubt that, in him, we have righteousness, for he made atonement for our sins. Knowing this, let us expect God to continue his work through our Redeemer—to continue and to add to it more and more, until he brings it to its end and final outcome.

Now let us cast ourselves down before the majesty of our good God, acknowledging our faults and asking him to make us feel them and love them less and less. Beholding ourselves in the death and passion of our Lord Jesus Christ, may we learn to hate ourselves and grieve for our offences. May we not doubt that because God's Son delivered us from all our guilt, we may now come before the majesty of God his Father, to be welcomed as his children, unworthy though we are to be reckoned among his creatures. And by this same power may we fight hard against all our failings and evil desires, so that we are made to partake of the forgiveness of our sins. May we be so strengthened that we live all our lives in conformity with God's will, and according as he has been gracious to us, may we try to please him in all obedience.

6

THE TRAVAIL OF HIS SOUL

He will see the travail of his soul and will be satisfied; by his knowledge my righteous servant will justify many, whose iniquity he will bear (Isa. 53:11).

THE prophet has added this verse in order to confirm what he had previously said, which was that the death of God's Son had not been in vain but would yield outstanding fruit for the salvation of the world. Here, however, he has more to say than he has said before. First, he reveals the love that Jesus Christ bore us, declaring that *he will be satisfied*, since by his death he has obtained eternal life for us. In the second place he makes it clear that Jesus Christ will not only suffer in his body, but also in his soul.

Now we know that the word 'satisfy' or 'make content' implies a strong desire. Many things happen which fail to move us; they are soon past and gone. They may even be to our advantage, but this does not mean that there we rest. A person may have many things but may not be content. He may not have the thing that matters most, or he may not have everything he wants. Here, however, the prophet declares that the Son of God will be wholly satisfied when he sees that he has acquired his church for himself, and that poor sinners have been rescued from the curse which was upon them. Being reconciled to God, they have obtained heaven as their inheritance.

In brief, we see here that our Lord Jesus Christ had no thought for himself but was carried away by the love he bore us; he found there his entire satisfaction, as if this was his sole desire, his sole motive and concern. Again, we must note that our hope will not be disappointed as long as we seek by faith the grace which Jesus Christ has won for us, and which is daily offered to us in the gospel. For the prophet tells us that *he will see*, showing that God has not only revealed his mercy to us in his Son, by giving him up to death for our sake; he will also ensure through his Holy Spirit that this death will not be fruitless. Many will understand and will know by experience that his suffering was not without purpose or in vain.

Let us open the door, then, to our Lord Jesus Christ, so that through him we may share in the fruit of his death and passion; let us draw near to him by faith. And let us not doubt that when we open our hearts to him, God will add this gift to all the rest, that just as he chose his Son to be our Redeemer, so he will grant us truly to enjoy the benefits he has brought us. This is what we have to remember about this verse.

There is a second point which we drew to your attention. Not only was Jesus Christ destined to be stricken, smitten and afflicted by his Father's hand, in order to suffer the punishment which we deserved; he was also destined to suffer distress of soul. Scripture does not merely say that he will see fruit from his beatings, afflictions and death, as the prophet had previously said. It tells us that *he will see the travail*—or *trials—of his soul*. The word Isaiah uses has this meaning. What he therefore says is that Jesus Christ not only endured severe torment in his body before being crucified; he had to go much further, suffering for us grief and the pangs of death. To all of this he submitted, so that we might be justified.

What would have happened if our Lord Jesus had been seen to suffer, but only in the eyes of men? If he had suffered only in his body, he would be the Redeemer of our bodies, but nothing more. But because we look to him chiefly for the confident assurance that death is no longer deadly to us, since we are delivered from God's curse, it was necessary for him to experience the pangs of death itself, and for him to come before God as a wretched offender might come before his judge. Our sin, we know, means not only death in point of time—that is, the parting of body and soul. It means the recognition that God is against us, and the feeling of terror at his judgment. And what is that like? It is a thing we simply cannot bear, a thing too awful for words.

Our Lord Jesus had thus to go to this extreme in order to acquit us. So says the prophet. Here we are given an even better view of God's great love for us, of the treasures of his grace and of the boundless goodness he has shown us. Here too we come to understand how careful and how zealous our Lord Jesus Christ was for our salvation, since he did not spare himself, and since he not only answered in his body to make atonement for our sins but underwent the terrors of one destined to feel God's judgment. He grasped the full force of the curse uttered by God's mouth, a curse which buries us in hell, a chasm in which we utterly perish.

Jesus Christ had to feel all this. Indeed, when we see that he sweated water and blood and that the angels had to descend to comfort him (Luke 22:43-44), we must confess that his grief was extreme: it was an example never before witnessed on earth. That is what is meant by the travail or trials of the soul of Jesus Christ. It is true, as Peter says, that the pangs of death could not hold him (Acts 2:24). Even so he had to fight hard against them. He was victorious, but it was not without an intense struggle and a great deal of difficulty.

What this passage teaches us is that although we must die, the death of our Lord Jesus Christ was not ineffectual, and that it benefits us according to our need. For death, to which we are now subject, serves to warn us of God's curse. If we were quite exempt from death, we would not know the grace won for us by our Lord Jesus Christ. We know how necessary it is for us to humble ourselves and for God to make us always feel his wrath. Although he wills to deliver us from it, we ought to think about it, to groan on account of our sins and to extol him even more for his mercy. Hence, while death is common to us all, it is not, strictly speaking, deadly for those who trust in Jesus Christ: they merely pass out of this world in order to live for God. In dying, therefore, we have reason to be comforted, knowing that God will be favourable to us and will turn evil into good, causing death, which before was a mortal wound, to serve as medicine.

Now how is that possible? It is because we no longer fear that God will judge us with utmost rigour and display his vengeance against us, provided we have Jesus Christ to mediate between us, and to show that he has made atonement for us. So in death there is no more that dreadful fear which fills us with dismay and causes us to despair. Instead, we can come freely and place ourselves in God's hands. Because Jesus Christ is said to have commended his spirit to God his Father (Luke 23:46), we know that in doing this he made himself the guardian of our souls. We can thus commit them with assurance into his hands, for he declared that nothing of all that had been given to him would perish (John 6:39; 10:28; 17:12).

That, then, is what we gain from the deep distress suffered by our Lord Jesus Christ. In addition to the death he endured and to the other torments, he experienced the terror of feeling that God was his judge, as if all the agonies of hell were his to suffer. This did not detract from the majesty of the Son of God; on the contrary it teaches us how greatly he prized our salvation, how dear we were to him and how precious our souls. Although he became as nothing, and had, as we saw before, neither form nor appearance that we should desire him, his self-abasement raised him all the higher. In fact, while God displayed his infinite loftiness and majesty in the creation of the world, in our Lord's death and passion we have even better cause to glorify God, in that Jesus Christ humbled himself and gave up his rights for us and for our salvation. And while he did not abandon his divine majesty, it was hidden for a time and was not obvious to men. This is what the prophet is referring to when he speaks of our Lord's distress. We thus learn that he forgot about himself, as it were, and had no concern for himself, for he had dedicated himself solely to our salvation. He answered for us both in his body and his soul and stood surety for us. We can clearly see, then, how godless and faithless those riff-raff are who want to suppress this truth. They are like mastiff dogs which bark without knowing why. Those pious frauds in popery, though ignorant of these things at least in part, are nevertheless obliged to confess that Jesus Christ felt real dread and terror. Admittedly they cannot define what it all meant, but they chatter on about it.

Here, on the other hand, there are scoundrels who are more monkish than those who dwell in the caves and brothels from which they came, bringing their putrid infection into God's church. Without a doubt that rabble who today are known as ministers and who are busy in that role, make God's church a pigsty. They are dogs devoid of religion; they make every effort to wipe from human memory all of God's grace and all that our Lord Jesus has done for us.[1] So when we see how Satan

[1] Calvin rarely identifies by name those he criticizes. It is likely that he is referring here to certain members of Geneva's Italian church who held unorthodox views regarding the Trinity and, more particularly, the person of Christ. Calvin had been in dispute with them since May 1558, and his attempt, supported by the city council, to secure their agreement to a common confession of faith, had had only partial success. Cf. his letter of 19 July 1558 to the Marquis of Vico, in John Calvin, *Tracts and Letters*, ed. Henry Beveridge and Jules Bonnet, 7 vols (Edinburgh: Banner of Truth Trust, 2009), VI:442-44.

drives them on and that they are as brazen as whores, we should be all the more careful to maintain this article of faith, namely that Jesus Christ was condemned by Pilate, an earthly judge, so that we might be absolved before God his Father. Not only was he crucified so that we might be delivered from the curse; not only did he suffer death so that we might be free of it; all this was to ensure that we had peace of conscience, might rejoice to feel God's fatherly love for us and might call upon him with full voice, knowing that he will receive us and that we will be acceptable to him.

It was therefore necessary that Jesus Christ should be plunged into the terrors he experienced and be treated as a wretched criminal. It was necessary that he who was the spotless Lamb of God, the mirror and model of all holiness and perfection, should answer for us and go surety for us, to the extent that he was condemned to the deepest hell. These pains he overcame and vanquished, as we have said, but he first had to fight hard. That is Isaiah's meaning here.

We read that, having borne his soul's travail, he was content, fully satisfied if, by this means, we might be redeemed. Today we should take fresh heart, conscious that if, through true obedience of faith, we accept the priceless blessing obtained for us by Jesus Christ, we can be sure that nothing that he suffered was in vain. How much less excuse, then, will there be for our ingratitude, if we do not come to him with fervent zeal and enjoy his gift of reconciliation with his Father, who is ready to welcome us as his children. That is something to remember about this verse.

Next it is said that *by his knowledge my Servant will justify many*. 'My righteous Servant,' the prophet says. The word 'servant', as we saw, in no way diminishes the majesty of our Lord Jesus Christ, for although he was Lord of every creature, he obtained new mastery as the Mediator who shared our very nature. Paul points to this in the second chapter of Philippians, which we have already noted in part: 'He chose to become a servant, and in that condition he humbled himself' (Phil. 2:7-8). 'Servant of God' is thus no empty title. We should not think that this is strange: it is much more strange that he who is the Son of God and who, as we read in John 17, is equal in glory with the Father (John 17:5), should be the servant of men, and should have so abased himself as to choose to serve. Yet that is how it was. That also is why he says, 'I am among you as one who serves, not as one who is master' (Matt. 20:28). Consequently, because Jesus Christ stooped so low that he became the servant of men, it is only right that here he is called God's servant. Otherwise, according, I mean, to God's decree, he could not have redeemed us, as we said before. (God was quite capable of saving us without any means at all, but we must always presume that it was necessary for Jesus Christ to obtain life for us.)[2] Now in order to do this he had to make himself a servant, otherwise he could not have rendered obedience to God his Father; and without that obedience he could not have made up for our transgressions and iniquities. That is why he is specifically called 'servant'—'righteous servant', in fact.

In short, what the prophet means is that we are rebels against God, and we remain so until he has remade us by his Holy Spirit. Even after he has touched our hearts with love for him, we are unprofitable servants (Luke 17:10): we trip up at every step, and when we think that the service we have given should be acceptable to him, it is never beyond reproach; it even deserves to be refused. Hence to wipe away our sins, Jesus Christ had to render to God agreeable service and obedience—that is to say, true satisfaction. We must understand, therefore, that he justifies us not only because he is God, but by virtue of his obedience in

[2] God's decree, that atonement should be made through the incarnate Son, rules out the possibility of his choosing any other means, compatible though such a choice would be with his sovereign freedom. Hence *nous avons toujours à présupposer* ...: 'we must always presume ...'. See above, Sermon 5, p. 85, note 2.

taking our nature upon himself, and in seeking in that nature to fulfil the law. This we could not do, for it was a burden designed to crush us all and to break our necks. We are justified by our Lord Jesus Christ because he resigned his rights for the sake of our salvation and was obedient to God his Father.

The prophet speaks in particular of 'knowledge', signifying that it was not enough for Jesus Christ himself to fulfil all that was needed for our salvation: we must lay hold of it by faith. How many unbelievers do we see for whom our Lord's death and passion mean harsher condemnation, because they trample on his sacred blood and reject the grace which is offered them? So although our Lord Jesus Christ is like the serpent lifted up in the wilderness, that all who were sick might be healed (Num. 21:8-9), we ourselves can gain nothing from him unless it be through knowledge. For in the wilderness, it was necessary to look at the bronze serpent; without that look the serpents' bite was fatal. In the same way the gospel is like a stage which lifts our Lord Jesus Christ high, or it is like a banner which shows him visibly to us and which allows us to look on him from afar. In sum, there is no darkness when, as Paul says, the gospel is preached (2 Cor. 4:6). In it we behold the grace of God which is revealed in our Lord Jesus Christ, otherwise our eyes must remain blindfolded by Satan.

At any rate attend carefully to what is said here: it is only by his knowledge that Jesus Christ justifies. It was of course necessary that the substance of our salvation should precede everything else, for when Scripture says that we are justified by faith, it does not exclude Jesus Christ or God's mercy. Faith is meant to guide us and to lead us forward. We will have a better understanding of this point, however, if we first note that we are not righteous in ourselves, for we must borrow our righteousness from somewhere else. If we were able to lead so disciplined a life that in every respect it matched the law and will of God, we would deserve to be accepted by him. Why? Because God must acknowledge goodness of which he is the fountainhead, otherwise he would not be true to himself. So if we patterned our lives on God's law and achieved the perfection it demands, we would undoubtedly be righteous through our works and, as Paul argues, we would have no need of Jesus Christ (Gal. 5:4). On the other hand, when we are obliged to borrow our righteousness from our Lord Jesus Christ and to seek it from him, this means that we are destitute of it. We thus conclude that since Scripture says that we must come to Jesus Christ, all are condemned on account of sin. God clearly shows that in ourselves we are wholly cursed. So much for that point.

To be sure the philosophers of old spoke a great deal about virtue.[3] It was commonly believed that we ought to please God by living decently. Yet what good did all that do? The very best of men, and those deemed to be entirely above reproach, were merely hypocrites, while others were given to evil in every form. Those who fancied that they were the cleverest and who were celebrated above everyone else, were nevertheless desperately flawed. Let men, then, presume as much as they like, let them reflect on how to lead a virtuous life. When they have done everything they can, when laws and rules have been put in place to give them guidance, they will never by this means be righteous in God's sight. This is because sin is rooted in us and cannot be cleansed by purely human remedies.

In short, we will never be justified by attending the schools of men, however much they teach what virtue is. God, moreover, has made known his law, in which is true and perfect righteousness. It is as Moses says: 'Behold, I proclaim good and evil to you; I show you the path of life' (Deut. 30:15). Can the law, then, justify us? Can it so discipline us that God accepts our life as

[3] The field of candidates is large, but doubtless includes Plato and Aristotle among the Greeks, and Cicero and Seneca among the Romans.

holy and righteous? No, quite the opposite! The law produces only death (2 Cor. 3:7); it makes us doubly guilty of condemnation; it inflames God's wrath.[4] These are the words which holy Scripture uses of it. So since the law cannot in itself justify us, how can men by their teaching, their rules and regulations, lead us to true righteousness?

If we ask how it is that God's law cannot justify and why, I have already mentioned the reason. It is true that in his law God shows what we could and should do to attain life, if we were such that there was nothing on our side to impede us. God's law therefore speaks, but it does not remake our hearts. When God tells us, 'This is what I ask of you,' if all our feelings, desires and thoughts are opposed to what he commands, we are not only condemned, but, as I said, the law makes us all the guiltier before God. Prior to the law we would have sinned through ignorance; but now we knowingly resist God, so that we seem to want to defy him. We know that the servant who is aware of his master's will but who fails to do it will suffer double punishment. That is why the law is said to work only wrath (Rom. 4:15). It makes God's anger burn all the hotter against us now that we have been taught it; it brings us death. How does it do that? It does it by making us see that we are condemned and lost. Does not the law proclaim life? No, life is not something we can attain. There must thus be another way for us to be justified, which is through the gospel.

In the gospel, God does not say, 'You must do this and that.' He says instead, 'Believe that my only-begotten Son is your Redeemer; embrace his death and passion as the remedy for all your ills. Steep yourselves in his blood and he will wash you; you will be made clean. Rely on the sacrifice he offers you, and you will be righteous.' The gospel thus brings us back to our Lord

[4] The fact that, as sinners, we are doubly guilty before God, is explained in the following paragraph.

Jesus Christ and bids us seek all righteousness in him, for by God's mercy he has atoned for us. That is how we can be justified by his knowledge. Paul demonstrates this in the tenth chapter of Romans, where he contrasts two sorts of righteousness, one through the law, the other through faith (Rom. 10:4-10). He affirms that righteousness can indeed be had through the law, when it says, 'He who does these things will live by them' (Lev. 18:5). It is certainly true that if we were able to fulfil all of God's commands, and if our lives were so well ordered that they had no spot or fault, God promised to accept us as righteous. Our reward would be assured, and we would not be disappointed.

As regards the law, this is quite certain. Yet who actually does what the law commands? We do the very opposite, and as I said before, we seem to want to defy God. Observe, then, that the door is shut against us so far as righteousness through the law is concerned: all that is left to us is God's curse. The gospel, by contrast, says this: 'Behold, this word is in your heart and in your mouth' (Rom. 10:8). What Paul means is that, in order to have the word in our heart and in our mouth, we must come to Jesus Christ. He is the one who by his Holy Spirit writes and inscribes in us the message of salvation, a message which would otherwise be drummed into our ears uselessly and to no avail. So since our Lord Jesus Christ puts his word into our hearts, pray that he may graciously grant us a pure, free disposition, so that we may seek in him all that we lack. This is how we will be justified by his knowledge, for there is no question that we could atone for ourselves to God in any way which might satisfy him. There is no question that, in giving an account of ourselves to God, we should say to him, 'Lord, we deserve to be accepted by you.' Not that, but this: 'We are poor sinners, bound to face your judgment. We cannot atone by ourselves. We must acknowledge that Jesus Christ alone is sufficient to make satisfaction.' So we will confess these things in all humility, admitting that we are wretched creatures, lost and damned until our Lord puts forth his hand to rescue us from the pit and chasm of hell.

Have we made that confession? We know also that our Lord Jesus Christ makes up for everything we lack. If we are defiled and full of filth, his blood will wash us and make us clean. If we are immersed in debt, not only to God but to Satan as to our adversary, payment has been made by the death and passion of God's Son. If we are foul and abhorrent to God, the sacrifice which our Lord Jesus has made has a pleasing aroma, so that all the evil in us is wiped away. This is how we are justified by the knowledge of Jesus Christ.

The first thing we learn from this teaching is that we do not have to go far to seek our righteousness: we find it in Jesus Christ himself, according as he took our nature and made himself our brother. This is a highly important point, for if we had to be justified by the divine essence of Jesus Christ, we would be far removed from his righteousness; we could never attain it. Since, however, it is said that the righteousness he gives us was accomplished in his human nature, we are able to come to him in a more intimate way. That too is why Satan has tried to muddle this truth. There are madmen who have dreamed up the idea that it is as God that our Lord Jesus Christ justifies believers. But then, as I said, we would have to go very far indeed to seek our righteousness. We would surely lose heart and faint before we ever reached him. On the contrary, it is because he became mortal man and made himself our Mediator that he calls us to himself: that is where we must seek our righteousness. That is one thing we need to notice.[5]

[5] Calvin here alludes to the doctrine of 'essential righteousness' formulated by the Lutheran theologian Andreas Osiander (1498–1552), but opposed by other coreligionists, including Melanchthon. Osiander viewed justification in terms not of imputation but of infusion, declaring that Christ's righteousness is ours by virtue of his divine nature, not by virtue of the sacrifice for sin which, as man, he offered on the cross. The Son's divine essence, he held, indwells the believer, who is thus *made*, rather than *reckoned*, righteous. See Calvin's lengthy critique in *Inst.* III.11.5-12.

Let us come back, however, to the word 'knowledge'. Because unbelievers shut the door to themselves and forfeit the blessing which they ought to receive through our Lord Jesus Christ, let us have attentive ears so that we accept the testimony given to us in the gospel. This is what Paul says in the verse we cited yesterday, that Jesus Christ, who did not know what sin was, became sin for us (2 Cor. 5:21). The gospel achieves that very thing today. 'We are,' says Paul, 'ambassadors for Jesus Christ. We beg you to be reconciled to God' (2 Cor. 5:20). Here Paul describes a twofold reconciliation. The first is that achieved by Jesus Christ himself, when he was made a sacrificial offering for us. The other is that which we attain each day by faith, when God tells us that although we have displeased him, he is always ready to forget all our wrongs and to tread them underfoot, provided we accept the benefit he offers us.[6]

Let us learn, therefore, to cherish the knowledge of the gospel more than we do. We should understand that through it we can share in the death and passion of our Lord Jesus Christ, for we are grafted into his body and made members of him. All that he has, we have in common with him; it is conveyed to us by the gospel. For that reason, Paul calls the gospel 'the power of God for salvation to all who believe' (Rom. 1:16). He thus shows that if we refuse to be saved by the gospel, it is as if we were rejecting the salvation that God wished to gain for us in and through his Son, and to which he daily invites and calls us. That, in short, is something we should notice.

We ought to value the gospel much more when we realize that in popery it has been veiled—no, completely blotted out!—so that poor souls are left famished. For although there is preaching after a fashion, people remain in a miserable state of

[6] It should be noted that while Calvin basically defines justification as the free imputation to sinners, by faith, of Christ's righteousness, the term covers a wide semantic field. In *Inst.* III.11.2, 4, for example, he treats terms such as 'reconciliation', 'acceptance' and 'remission of sins' as synonymous with justification.

doubt and misgiving. No one ever has assurance of God's favour. The papists even say that it would be presumptuous to be certain of God's love: we can only resort to guesswork![7] That, however, is to destroy the fruit of our Lord's death and passion. Let us learn, therefore, to make the most of the gospel, so that we may have the assurance that God loves us and accepts us as his very own children. So as I said, let us cherish and exalt his grace all the more, when we see how distant most people are from it.

Here then are the prophet's words: 'He lay down his soul for many.' His meaning is that we are not justified by faith if, on the basis of some idle thought, we believe that God exists, and if we have some vague, general notion that Jesus Christ suffered and died. No, we are justified by faith only because we come to share in his sacrificial offering, and look to God to be favourable to us and not to impute our sins and iniquities to us.

The papists are so dull and senseless that, in trying to show that we are not justified by faith alone, they argue like this: 'We are justified by God's mercy, so it is not by faith alone.' Or again: 'We are justified by the death and passion of our Lord Jesus Christ, so it is not by faith alone.' It is the same as saying: 'We are made warm by the heat, so it is not the sun. We are illumined by the light, so it is not the sun.' Understand that when Scripture speaks of faith, it is seeking to bring us back to the gospel, for, as I said before, there are two kinds of righteousness. The law tells us that we will be righteous if we fulfil all that God commands. But success is impossible, so that we are devoid of righteousness, utterly excluded from it. The other kind of righteousness is to be found in Jesus Christ, when, after carefully examining ourselves, we are persuaded of our wickedness and feel only dread, knowing

[7] The Council of Trent, in the ninth chapter of its decree on justification (January 1547), asserted that, while no pious person ought to doubt the mercy of God, 'each one, when he considers his own weakness and indisposition, should have fear and apprehension concerning his own grace, since no one can know with the certainty of faith … that he has obtained the grace of God.'

that God is arming himself with vengeance against us: he has only to thunder to strike us down. When we reach that point, that extreme moment of crisis, look, Jesus Christ appears to present us with a cure which will relieve all our pains. He assures us that he alone is sufficient to help us attain the salvation he has won for us. That is how we are justified by faith.

Isaiah thus says exactly what Paul was to say in later years. We must first come to the death and passion of our Lord Jesus Christ and behold him crucified for us. Next, through the gospel we must gain assurance that what he did and suffered belongs to us and applies to us today, since the Father will not allow his death to be unavailing. It is meant to be a powerful, effective sacrifice which bears fruit in us each day. That is the message of this verse.

Knowledge of our Lord Jesus Christ is no empty thing, as it is for many who, when we speak to them about knowing the gospel, think that it is enough to have some fleeting idea of what is taught. Knowledge implies that we should firmly believe Jesus Christ to be the sole author of our salvation. This cannot happen unless we keenly feel that in ourselves we are lost, and that God, who is willing to receive us once and for all in his mercy, will give effect to his wish. Now it is impossible for us to attain such knowledge unless we are illumined by the Holy Spirit. To be illumined by him is an unmistakable sign that God desires to work in us, making us possessors of his righteousness from which we were once a long way off. Thus God sees to it that the gospel is proclaimed. Even so, this is not enough. It is all double Dutch to us, as we say, until we are inwardly touched by the Holy Spirit. From this comes our faith. It is then that we become good and true disciples of Jesus Christ and experience the fruit of his teaching. That is what the prophet points out here.

Once more Isaiah declares that Jesus Christ has borne our sins, to show that atonement is in him, and that our sins would be a burden crushing us in the depths of hell if he had not relieved us of them. For what is meant by sin, if not the wrath of God? God has only to lift a finger to make an end of all of us. As Scripture says, at his mere breath the rocks flow down and the mountains melt and run like wax (Psa. 97:5). If God gives the slightest sign of his wrath and fury, there is nothing so solid in the world which does not melt. What, then, will become of us who are such frail creatures, if God should show the stern face of a judge and should call us to account? We will not need to hear a word issuing from his mouth: the merest sign by which he summons us to judgment will be a bottomless chasm which swallows us whole. Our sins are therefore a burden which we cannot bear. They are infinite in number; we do not have the shoulders to support them and to stand beneath their weight.

As for Jesus Christ, however, while he suffered in the weakness of his flesh, he was always sustained by the power of the Holy Spirit who had been given to him. That is how he triumphed even on the cross, as Paul writes in Colossians (Col. 2:15). We must keep coming back to the prophet's words, which are well explained by Peter in his first letter: 'He bore our sins upon the tree' (1 Pet. 2:24). It was not of course the strength of the wood which helped our Lord bear our sins; he bore them on the tree, for he was crucified, cursed as it were by God; he bore the entire curse in which we were immersed. He accepted all these things so that we might feel their fruit, and might now enjoy the victory in which, through him, we share.

So if we ourselves are burdened, let us come to Jesus Christ and find relief. And let us recognize the means he uses: he delivers us from all our debts. We must no longer imagine that we can offer God any satisfaction or recompense when he calls us to account. This must always be our starting point: our utter shame. Nor should we doubt that we are now unburdened, for

Jesus Christ has borne our load. We can now lift up our heads, knowing that he has freed us from God's judgment.

Given, then, that we have been sanctified once and for all by the sacrifice offered by Jesus Christ when, as he himself declared, he dedicated himself to God's service (John 4:34; 5:30), we must today lay all our sins on him and seek full righteousness in him. In order to do this, we must lend an attentive ear to the gospel, knowing that God invites us to himself with kindly words. He does not demand from us things which are impossible, and which could only drive us to despair. The law indeed pronounced a curse on those who failed to fulfil all these things (Deut. 27:26; Gal. 3:10). In effect, this excluded us entirely from salvation. Here, however, we are told that if we are miserable sinners, God applies the appropriate remedy: we can be justified by our Lord Jesus Christ. As poor beggars who are in utter want, we come seeking help.

Furthermore, we are reminded that our Lord Jesus Christ is righteous: he justifies us in that he took our nature upon himself, so that we might approach God personally and enjoy so great a blessing. Let us not say, 'Who will ascend above the clouds?' Paul, citing this verse from Moses (Rom. 10:6; Deut. 30:12), affirms that when the gospel is preached to us, we do not have to run far afield to learn that God is close to us. That would be like pulling Jesus Christ from his heavenly throne! Similarly, we are not to say, 'Who will descend to the depths?' (Rom. 10:7), for our Lord went down there, thus assuring us that he has rescued us and now fulfils the office of Mediator. He wants us to share in his righteousness, to be clothed in it and to make it our own so that it dwells in us. He wants it to fill us and to lift us up to God his Father. On him we call, doubting nothing.

Now let us cast ourselves down before the majesty of our good God, acknowledging our faults and begging him so to make us feel them that we rightly repent of them. May he correct them day by day, and may we so grow that we are made one with his perfect righteousness, which must continually be our goal and the thing for which we yearn. May we exalt the grace of our Lord Jesus Christ and place our trust in it. May we not wander in our idle fancies or in the deceits which Satan sets before us, and which still today lead poor folk astray. May we know that fullness of salvation lies in our Lord alone; may we so possess him that we are content with him, and he with us. And may the benefits of his death and passion be always ours.

7

OUR ADVOCATE AND INTERCESSOR

Therefore I will divide his spoils with the great, and he will share his booty with the strong, for he poured out his soul in death and was reckoned among the transgressors. He bore the sin of many, and he prayed for the unrighteous (Isa. 53:12).

HERE the prophet declares in essence that our Lord Jesus Christ not only vanquished death by dying, but also earned the right to take his enemies' goods from them and to seize their spoils. That is what follows once victory has been won. It is true that our Lord did not become rich by acquiring this world's wealth; but it was for this purpose, as we have said, that he fought with death.

It was necessary, as we know, for Satan, the prince of this world, to be driven from his dominion, otherwise ours would have been a more than sorry state. It was necessary, too, that sin should no longer have the upper hand. In this way, then, our Lord Jesus Christ despoiled his enemies, ensuring that we are under Satan's tyranny no more, nor are we in bondage to sin. We have been set free. Accordingly, Paul shows how this verse in the psalm he cites has been fulfilled: 'God ascended on high and took captivity captive' (Eph. 4:8; Psa. 68:18). God took and throttled his enemies who were powerless to resist him, and received homage from men, together with their tribute.

Of course, David in this psalm spoke figuratively of God's ascent on high. It was because God had for a time seemed not to notice, appearing to have gone to sleep. Things were in such disarray that the faithful groaned in their helplessness, whereas the wicked were free to enjoy themselves. Thus, when there is so much trouble in the world, and when calling upon God seems to get us nowhere, God appears to be somehow cowed and hidden. On the other hand, when he upholds the church's cause by destroying its enemies, David speaks of God as ascending on high. Paul affirms that this was fulfilled by Jesus Christ in that, for a time, his majesty was veiled, and men thought nothing of him. So, says Paul, he had to descend to the earth's very depths and to be despised by men, in order finally to be exalted, receiving from men not merely homage but also the right to divide their spoils and tributes. For whereas in the psalm it is said that he took the tributes which were due to him as to one who had overcome his enemies, Paul says that he gave his gifts generously to men.

At first glance there might seem to be a discrepancy between these two things. They are quite consistent, however, in the sense that our Lord Jesus Christ was not personally enriched. It was not for his sake, for he needs nothing: it was so that he might divide the spoils among us. As the psalm declares, not only will those who have fought share in the booty, but also the women who never left home (Psa. 68:12). We know indeed how fully God has blessed us through the death and passion of his only Son. Not that we are strong or industrious in ourselves: we are less so than the women who are busy spinning with their distaffs while we are away at war! When, therefore, it is said that *God will give to Jesus Christ the spoils of his enemies*, strong and powerful though they are, it does not apply to him alone. It is meant to teach us that the devil has no rights or privileges over us, once we have come to share in the death and passion of God's Son. This we obtain through the gospel.

Let us submit, then, to our Lord Jesus Christ. Let us acknowledge him as our King and let there be no pretence about it. It is certain that we will obtain from him, first, freedom, and after that the good things which we need but which we utterly lack, unless we receive them from his hand. Think of just how wretched we would be if Satan had not been despoiled. We are his to possess; he enjoys us in all tranquillity, as our Lord himself says (John 8:44). We are, so to speak, his possession and domain. We need our Lord's death and passion to produce their fruit in us; we need our enemies to be defeated and at the same time put to flight; we need Jesus Christ to plant his foot on their throats so that, whatever mischief they may plot against us, they are powerless.

When our text speaks of *the strong*, of those who excel in vigour, it is so that we should not dread all the might, arms and trappings of our enemies. They are bound to scare us when we consider our own weakness, and when we remember that the devil is a roaring lion (1 Pet. 5:8) and that sin has complete sway over us. These things, I say, might well terrify us, if we did not have Scripture's testimony that there is neither power nor fortress nor anything else which prevents our Lord Jesus Christ from seizing his enemies' spoils and from routing them. He so strips them of all that they have, that the things which once were loss to us now become gain.

Now this is true not only of Satan, the head of all the wicked, but of all our adversaries. As many unbelievers as there are, so many are our foes. They rage against us, and the whole world, as we see, is opposed to us. How then would we fare if Jesus Christ was unable to overcome all who are so mighty and so strong?

The first thing to remember about this verse is that Jesus Christ, having ascended, now not only holds our enemies captive and bound, but has taken possession of their booty. We have now received the gifts presented in homage to him, so that we who are poor and needy might be enriched by his generosity.

In particular, we are told that the spoils are his *because he poured out his soul in death*. Once more Isaiah explains that our Lord Jesus Christ offered himself of his own free will. The words 'poured out' indicate that he did not spare himself, nor did he act reluctantly. Anyone who is compelled to give will finally open his hand, but he will always display a certain meanness. The person, on the other hand, who spreads his gifts abroad, gives proof of a free and willing heart. We therefore learn that our Lord Jesus Christ burned with such love for us that his life was poured out like water. He offered himself as a voluntary sacrifice, to demonstrate that his only wish was to reconcile us to God his Father. He sought to give us greater assurance that by coming to him, we should not doubt that God will receive us with every kindness. How could our Lord reject us and cut us off, since he had ventured all regardless by pouring out his soul? Hearing these things, we have every reason to come to him more freely, and to know that he will make good the sacrifice which, in his boundless love for us, he offered to God his Father.

For the rest, because the fruit of our Lord's death and passion is everlasting, we understand that today we are as much enriched as we need to be, and as experience confirms, for he is bound to aid us in all the necessities which surround us. Otherwise, what would we do if his hand were not always ready to uphold us? We would assuredly find life impossible. As it is, he gives us quite enough to remedy all our needs.

All of the Holy Spirit's gifts are part of the spoils belonging to our Lord Jesus Christ. God his Father enriched him with them, since we were bereft of them, and since the devil was preventing the Spirit's powers from taking effect among men. Now, however, those gifts have enriched us, for every impediment has been removed. As I have said, now that Jesus Christ has despoiled our enemies, everything which in this world was opposed to us has been made to serve us and our salvation.

That said, the prophet now declares that *he was reckoned among the transgressors, yet he bore the sins of many*. We have already noted how our Lord Jesus Christ bore the sins of many—by paying the penalty which we could on no account bear. Burdened by our sins, we would have been too frail to stand before God. There was no means of deliverance to be found anywhere on earth. Our Lord Jesus Christ had thus to relieve us by offering himself in our place and by bearing the burden of all our transgressions. These were imputed to him in the sight of God his Father, and he was required to make payment for them.

Now anyone who owes what he cannot pay is stooped and bent; his shoulders droop; he is uncertain what to do, for he carries a burden which, we might say, breaks him and wears him down. What then will become of us, for we are debtors not to a mortal creature but to the living God? And it is not a matter of silver or gold, but of our transgressions, which deserve his awful wrath, as Scripture makes clear. So the verdict of everlasting death is prepared for everyone, until our Lord Jesus Christ frees us from our load. How could we ever be equal to this if he who had the power to triumph over all had not stood in our place and made up for what we lacked? In this way, then, our Lord bore the sins and iniquities of many.

Now the word 'many' is often equivalent to 'all'. Sure enough, our Lord Jesus Christ was offered to everyone, for Scripture is not speaking of three or four when it says that God so loved the world that he did not spare his only Son (John 3:16; Rom. 8:32). Nevertheless, we should note the words which the Evangelist adds to this verse: 'so that whoever believes in him should not perish but have everlasting life'. That was how our Lord Jesus Christ suffered for all, and there is no excuse today for anyone, whether great or small, since it is in him that we have salvation. The faithless who turn away from him and who by their malice deprive themselves of him, are doubly guilty today. What pretext can they claim for their ingratitude, when they will not accept the blessing in which, by faith, they might share?

Observe, therefore, that even if we came in droves to our Lord Jesus Christ, we would not stop one another from finding him sufficient for every one of us. If it was a question of looking to a human being for relief, someone might say, 'Please bear this burden for me.' But if a second person came, or a hundred all at once, our man might dearly wish to relieve each and every one, but his back must surely stoop, since he would not be strong enough to shoulder all that load. Similarly, if we were hungry and thirsty and asked to borrow food and drink from someone, he might be able to do this for a dozen of us or so, but if we came in such great numbers that his provisions were all used up, he would soon run short. Thus, among men, when there are very many of us, many people are needed to give us help and relief. When, however, we come to Jesus Christ, we need not fear that his power will fail, and that when each of us has had his share, he himself will be diminished, and that there will not be enough for the rest. No, the more numerous the people who come, the richer we will find him in aiding us in our need.

Isaiah has good reason, then, to say that he bore the sins of many: this is to stop us envying our neighbours as if we were missing out on help, because there are too many others. That is the message of this verse.

'He was reckoned,' we are told, 'among the transgressors.' Remember first of all that our Lord Jesus Christ was hung between two thieves (Mark 15:17-18). He endured all the condemnation which we deserved, so that today we have a more certain and unmistakable pledge that we are absolved in God's sight of all our sins and offences. Mark thus cites this testimony of the prophet when he records that two thieves were hung along with our Lord Jesus Christ, showing that all men were bound to regard him with abhorrence, as they beheld the shame visited upon him—all this in order to deliver us today from God's wrath, and from the punishment our sins deserved. For instead of being plunged into the very depths of hell, we are now partners with the angels in heaven, who are dedicated to God's service and who fulfil all righteousness. This blessing is therefore ours, because our Lord was willing to take our place and to put himself among the guilty, choosing to court disgrace in the sight of men.

Consequently, the reproaches which he bore raise us on high, delivering us from all condemnation and ensuring that sin is no longer imputed to us. In what, after all, does our salvation consist, if not in the covering and blotting out of sin? We could never have obtained this by any other means, but only through the Son of God who, as Paul says, is our redemption (1 Cor. 1:30). He was, that is to say, the price and payment for what we owed: we are now clear and free of debt.

Isaiah thus has every reason to associate these two things, showing once more, as he has done before, that we have cause to glorify our Lord Jesus Christ, as we see the fruit which comes to us from the abuse to which he was exposed. If our Lord had done this only to demonstrate his humility, that would have been too small a thing. He did it so that we should find in him whatever we lack, and to provide a remedy for all that might burden us. When we are thus reconciled to God, when we obtain righteousness and have the assurance that our sins are pardoned, we no longer dread to come to Jesus Christ, even though at first glance his crucifixion appears disgraceful from a human point of view. We understand that he triumphed over sin and Satan, in order to win righteousness for us. He cancelled the bond which stood against us (Col. 2:14), enabling us now to come to God with sure proof that we are righteous. In this we can therefore openly boast, whereas before we shrank in fear when having to recognize our guilt. Such is the prophet's meaning.

Having said all this, Isaiah finally adds that *he prayed for the unrighteous*. What this statement shows is that, in his death and passion, Jesus Christ exercised the office of priest, without which we would not have all that we need to be sure of our salvation. It is true that, because our Lord's death and passion were the sacrifice by which our sins are washed away, because his blood is for our cleansing and because his obedience puts an end to our rebelliousness and obtains righteousness for us, all these things give us reason to rejoice. That, however, is not all there is, for Scripture says that if we call upon God's name we will be saved (Joel 2:32; Rom. 10:13). Yet how can we have access to God? How bold we would have to be in order to pray to him, and especially to address him openly as 'our Father'! Would it not be too presumptuous of us to pray to him familiarly, like that, and to boast that we are his children, unless there was someone who could speak for us? Where could we find an advocate or attorney who could have done this for us before we came to Jesus Christ? This is what the prophet means when he ends by saying, 'He prayed for the unrighteous.'

It is true that on the cross he asked his Father for pardon and grace for the very people who had persecuted him. 'Father,' he said, 'forgive them, for they do not know what they are doing' (Luke 23:34). That is one prayer uttered by the Lord Jesus for the unrighteous, and for his enemies who had treated him so cruelly and by whose hand he was crucified. The prophet, however, was not speaking only of this special prayer: rather he was pointing to our Lord's priesthood. He nevertheless had good reason to mention the unrighteous here, for earlier he had said that

Jesus Christ bore the sins of God's people and suffered for the iniquities of many. At this point, however, Isaiah ascribes a different title to those for whom Jesus Christ prayed; he calls them 'transgressors'.

Now in speaking of the people of God, the prophet aims to show that those deemed most excellent, most righteous, need to have their sins forgiven. This they can have only because our Lord shed his blood to wash them and to make them clean. So this is one point: if we want to belong to the church and to be recognized as members of God's flock, we must know that it is only because Jesus Christ is our Redeemer. We should not fear to come to him, however numerous we may be. Instead, each of us should draw his neighbours in, for he is sufficient to save every one of us.

Scripture therefore describes us as transgressors, to make us think hard about our sins, for we know hold bold and impetuous we are. As a result, we are very often more embarrassed and restrained when we ask a mere man for a favour than when we come before God. Here, then, the prophet strikes down our pride and haughtiness by calling us 'unrighteous'. It is as if he said: 'Unhappy souls, who are you to presume to call upon God and to address him as "Father"? From where do you derive this honour? Who would dare to come before the presence of God's majesty and say, "I am one of your children"?' 'Off you go,' God might say, 'and hide yourselves. You are all unrighteous, and when you come before me, you come before your judge. You should tremble and be utterly ashamed. There is, however, one remedy, one only which can save you. When you call upon my name, you have an impregnable fortress in the powerful intercession of the Mediator. Without that you have no hope of salvation, you are all lost in your sins. Recognize, then, how much you need my Son to mediate, to intercede for you and to fulfil the office of priest.'

This is why the prophet insists that we are all unrighteous and transgressors. He wants us to realize that the door is closed to us and that we are not worthy to approach God. All of us are overwhelmed and ruined unless we turn to Jesus Christ for refuge. Without this remedy we must rot and perish in our misery and wretchedness. Yet even when we are humbled in this way, we can still come to our Lord Jesus Christ, knowing that he is the one who speaks for us, and that through him we can freely call ourselves God's children. So when we come and pray, 'Our Father in heaven', we must acknowledge that our lips are unclean. We are not even worthy to call God our Creator. So much less, then, should we presume to call ourselves his children.

Be that as it may, our Lord Jesus Christ speaks on our behalf, and our prayers and supplications are sanctified by him. As is said in the last chapter of the letter to the Hebrews, it is through him that we give God the sacrifice of prayer and praise (Heb. 13:15), for he is our Mediator, and in his name we call upon God our Father. We can freely boast, therefore, that he will count us as his children. This is how we are meant to apply this verse.

Our Lord Jesus Christ gave proof of this when, as we read in the seventeenth chapter of John, he prayed for his own, saying: 'Holy Father, here are those whom you have given me. I am now leaving this world, but I have kept them, and none has perished except the son of perdition. Those whom you committed to my care I have preserved. I pray now for them, and not only for them but for all those who through their word will believe in me. I do not pray for the world, but for all whom you have given me, that you may bless and sanctify them, and that they may be one with us' (John 17:11-12, 17).

Now when we see that the Son of God prayed—yes, that he who is everlasting God should stoop so low that he begged and presented his requests to God on our behalf—should we not acknowledge his infinite kindness here? Let us first, then, remember what we have been told, that we only profane God's name when we call upon him, unless we do so in the name of Jesus Christ. For our lips are foul and unclean: we are corrupt through and through—verminous, indeed. But because our Lord so condescended as to beg and to represent us when he asked a favour of God his Father, we are firmly grounded and supported when we come to make our prayers today. Isaiah said that Jesus Christ prayed for the unrighteous. He too says that he prays, but not for the world itself or for those who are happy in their sins and who stubbornly continue in them. Such people are cut off from this blessing and privilege, which is reserved only for God's children. If, then, we remain in this world and are separated from Jesus Christ, the requests he made to God his Father do not belong to us; they are useless to us. Listen to what he says: 'I gave your word to them, and they believed. I pray for them, and not only for them—that is, his disciples—but for those who will believe their message' (John 17:8, 20).

Remember that today we are partners with the disciples and apostles of our Lord Jesus Christ, and that this prayer which he prayed only once will continue to benefit us, opening the way for all our supplications as long as we accept the gospel message with the obedience of faith. Today, then, we should have no doubts about how to make our requests. Knowing that he prayed this prayer, we should no longer say, 'How can we be sure that the power of his prayer can reach as far as us?' Let us believe the gospel and, following the disciples and apostles, we will be united with them. Will we call God's Son a liar, he who is the eternal and unchanging truth? With his own lips he declared that, gathered up in this prayer, are all who accept the teaching of the gospel; he has included them in it.

Accordingly, although for our part we are miserable offenders and thus unworthy of approaching God, when, through the gospel, we lay hold of the promises it contains, we can come before God, and not only be acceptable to him, since his only Son has interceded for us; we can also now call upon him, with Jesus Christ keeping us company. As he says: 'Here am I, with the servants whom you have given me' (Isa. 8:18; Heb. 2:13). He appears first, as is said in the eighth chapter of Isaiah, and then he brings all of his flock with him: 'those whom you have given me', he says. He declares there that he is ready to serve God his Father with all who have been given him. There is thus no doubt that we are all associated in this prayer, as in all of God's praises, which Jesus Christ intones, so to speak, as the first cantor and as the one who leads us in prayer. And because of him there is no voice which does not blend in so well that the melody in any way lacks harmony.

If our voices were in tune with those of the angels, that would already be an extraordinary privilege; but when the Son of God condescends to be on such intimate terms with us as to say, 'Come, I will lead you, I will speak for you,' should this not truly thrill us?

We find these things, moreover, foreshadowed in the law, when the chief priest not only offered sacrifices to God but accompanied them with prayers. Under these ancient shadowy forms, the priest could not intercede before God and be acceptable to him without the shedding of blood. With the blood, however, he combined prayers, seeking pardon for the people's sins and asking God to receive in mercy those who deserved to be rejected. Now as we see, Jesus Christ put an end to all the symbols of the law which he chose to fulfil in himself. Thus he offered his blood to wash away our sins; not the blood of calves or lambs as under the law, but his own sacred blood, consecrated by the Holy Spirit, so that through it we might have complete holiness (Heb. 9:12-14).

To the shedding of blood Jesus Christ also added prayers. That is why he is now called our Mediator, and why he is said to intercede for us. So when Paul speaks of prayers, he adds that there is one God, and one Mediator, a man, the Lord Jesus (1 Tim. 2:5). He might have said that there is one God, and that Jesus Christ is God's eternal Word, being of the same essence and having the same glory and majesty. He does not, however, speak in those terms. Having said that there is one God, he writes that there is one Mediator between God and man, the man Jesus Christ. It is as if he said, 'Here is the Son of God who, having clothed himself with our nature and having been made like one of us, except for sin, now intercedes for us.' Now the priests of old needed to pray for themselves—which they did—and then for the sins of the people, among whom they were included (Lev. 4:3-7; 16:15-19; Heb. 5:1-3; 7:27; 9:7). Our Lord Jesus, however, is exempt from this necessity: he does not need to ask to be forgiven for sins committed; he intercedes for us.

Hence in the eighth chapter of Romans, Paul encourages us to come boldly to God. He pointedly asks, 'Who can be against us?' While we have many enemies, we should not dread them, for to whom must we account for our lives? Who is our judge? It is Jesus Christ, and he is our Advocate who intercedes for us, and who is there to make peace between God and us. He is the one who will help us find grace. We can lift up our heads, therefore, with boldness, and present ourselves to God; we can dare to come before his judgment seat, since Jesus Christ stands between us. When Scripture speaks of intercession, this is what we must remember.

Whenever, then, the death and passion of Jesus Christ are proclaimed to us, let us add to them the prayer he prayed. He prayed it only once, but he meant it to endure and to have effect forever. There is no need today for him to kneel before God his Father in order to beg: Scripture teaches that he will always be our Intercessor. How is that possible? By virtue of his death and passion, and by virtue of the prayer he prayed. By virtue of these things our prayers are granted, just as if he were speaking still today on our behalf. All our prayers, as I said before, are consecrated by him, otherwise they would be unholy. Every time, in fact, believers prepare to pray to God—whereas the papists asperge themselves with holy water and mutter their spells and incantations and other such nonsense—they ought to feel that their prayers are sprinkled with the blood of Jesus Christ, so that they are clean and pure and accepted by God as a fragrant sacrifice. We should know, then, that our Lord Jesus Christ was not a priest for one day only, but that he still retains that office, and always will, and we will always feel the fruit of it.

If this were properly understood, people would not have gone to such extremes of superstition and wickedness, as has been the case. Nowadays, as we see, the papists are like poor wandering beasts who do not know which path or track to take when they pray to God. They have an endless number of patron saints and advocates, and each manufactures one for himself. True, they have many that they hold in common, but after all their so-called *kyrielles*, each pays his devotion to a saint of his own devising.[1] Thus Jesus Christ is robbed of his honour! Since they are not content with Jesus Christ, it is undoubtedly the devil who possesses them; he has driven them to such fury that in their spite against God they give to one saint or another the rightful office which he has given to Jesus Christ.

So today the papists call the Virgin Mary their advocate. The devil take their prayers! It is as if they were denying God and our Lord Jesus Christ! The Virgin Mary herself must cry vengeance against them, for they have made a hateful idol of her. They have stolen from Jesus Christ the dignity of his priesthood, which God ratified by a solemn oath, and they have set out to falsify all of holy Scripture. They firmly imagine that Mary will come

[1] *Kyrielles*: litanies consisting of petitions said by the priest, interspersed with set responses said by the people.

to their aid. Instead, as I said, she must cry vengeance against them for the wrong they have done her, for if they were to spit in her face and load her with reproaches, they could surely not insult her more than when they call her their advocate. Why so? Because Scripture affirms that Jesus Christ was appointed priest by God his Father. By what means? By a solemn oath. 'I have sworn,' he said, 'and I will not repent' (Psa. 110:4; Heb. 5:6; 7:17). It is on this that we should rely, that is, on the intercession of our Lord Jesus Christ, since, as Paul writes in the third chapter of Ephesians, we can draw near to God and can come before him, provided we are led to him by Jesus Christ; it is through him that we find grace (Eph. 3:11-12).

What, then, do the papists want to do? They want to abolish our Lord's priesthood and to make it null and void. Since they come so brazenly to overturn God's changeless decree, how can they hope to have their prayers answered? The only conclusion we can draw is that in popery all sound teaching has been buried. And why? I am well aware that they say we are not worthy to come before God. That is true, who doubts it? Nevertheless, let us consider where our worthiness might be found. Is it not found in Jesus Christ, and only in him? They, however, turn to the Virgin Mary, to St Michael or the apostles; then too they have the saints they have invented for themselves, saints who never lived on earth but who have been canonized by whim of the pope—yes, but only to end up in deepest hell! Those are their patron saints and advocates.

Still, supposing we conceded to the papists that their saints—who never existed or who were half-devils or ghosts!—were in fact apostles and martyrs who lived as holy lives as possible, did they not need an advocate as much as anyone else? Without question, the Virgin Mary could not have found grace in God's sight apart from the Head. She needed Jesus Christ to be her Redeemer, just as much as he is ours. The apostles and martyrs, the patriarchs and prophets were similarly obliged to turn to this Redeemer, who is common to all of us. Imagine if we went looking to them for help! They would send us back to our Lord Jesus Christ, telling us to make our way to him, and that he sweetly invites us, saying, 'Come to me.' So let us not retreat or wander off; let us freely draw near.

Our Lord speaks thus not only for the prophets' sake or for the sake of the apostles, the martyrs and the Virgin Mary. He seeks to gather all of us to himself, as is most necessary for us. Let us not, I say, wander about in our prayers to God, and let us acknowledge how good he has been in choosing to rescue us from the darkness and disarray of popery, and in teaching us that the door to him is open, since Jesus Christ is our Intercessor. Let us stick to him, without straying to one side or the other, for if our prayers are not governed by God's word, they are sure to be petty and God will reject them. Nor can they be made in faith, unless we are assured of God's truth. So if we want our prayers to be grounded in faith, they must be in keeping with God's will. We must follow his command, which is that we should claim Jesus Christ as our Intercessor, Advocate and Mediator. This is the direction which God bids us take, and the foundation on which we should rely, lest we sway like reeds in every wind.

For this reason our Lord so often says, 'Whatever you ask my Father in my name, will be given to you' (John 14:13; 15:16; 16:24). We know also that, under the law, believers, though not having the same light as we have today, did not fail to set forth Jesus Christ, according to the forms which had been given to them. 'Lord God,' they said, 'look upon the face of your Christ, and for the love of your Anointed hear our prayer' (Psa. 84:9). 'Lord God,' says Daniel, 'hear our prayer for our Lord's sake' (Dan. 9:17). The Psalms very often repeat this kind of statement. There, it is true, it is David who is spoken of, but that is because he represented our Lord Jesus Christ; and when Daniel says, 'for our Lord's sake', he clearly shows that he means the promised Redeemer, whose coming at that time was close.

Jesus Christ speaks more openly still, when he declares, 'Hitherto you have asked nothing in my name. Now ask, and it will be granted to you' (John 16:24). It is as if he were saying, 'Until now you did not know that I was to act as Mediator on your behalf with God my Father.' He had not yet ascended into heaven, nor had he even torn down the veil of the temple in order to give us access to God. Now, however, since the veil has been torn in two, we have personal access to him, and our Lord has entered, not into a material sanctuary as the priests did in the era of the law, but into heaven itself, in the majesty of God his Father, so that there we might find grace. God's throne is thus no longer a throne of majesty which fills us with dread: instead, he invites us gently and out of fatherly love, because we come in and through the name of the priest he has ordained for us.

In this way the intercession of Jesus Christ continually benefits us. It is an impregnable fortress, ensuring that when we come to him he will hear and answer us. We will find by experience that whoever calls upon the name of the Lord will be saved (Joel 2:32; Rom. 10:13). And although this utterance by the prophet Joel was made before our Lord's appearing, the faithful under the law made such good use of it that their example should serve to strengthen and assure us—us, I say, who witness the perfect fulfilment of all that was prefigured by the law. When, therefore, we come to God in prayer and call upon him in the name of him who is our Advocate, we will know in truth that he is always interceding for us, so that all that we request is granted to us.

Now let us cast ourselves down before the majesty of our good God, acknowledging our faults and praying that he may make us feel them more and more, so that we, humbling ourselves, may fight against them day by day and so be rid of them. May we seek to be clothed with his righteousness and enriched by the gifts of his Holy Spirit, and thus appear before him pure and blameless. And since we daily need to be reconciled to him through the Mediator, may we have grace to pray to him in sincere trust. May we lean upon him and embrace with firm faith the promise that he gives us, saying, 'Come to me, all you who labour and are heavy laden, and I will relieve you.' May we therefore know that the office of Mediator has not been given to him in vain, but that through him our prayers today are heard and answered; and may our requests be so hallowed and dedicated to God that he will accept and acknowledge them all.

PRAYERS ACCOMPANYING THE WEEKDAY SERMON

CALVIN'S sermons on Isaiah were preached, as we have seen, on weekdays. Except for the Sunday morning service and the midweek (Wednesday) service, which was designated a day of prayer, the Genevan liturgy of 1542 prescribed no set form of words for the prayers which preceded and followed the sermon. These were left to the minister's discretion. The prayers which follow are those which Calvin was accustomed to use in all weekday services but one, Wednesday. (Text in *CO* 23:741, 755–57.)

PRAYER FOR ILLUMINATION

Let us call upon our good God, that it may please him to cast his merciful and fatherly eye on us his poor servants, not imputing to us the many faults and offences by which we do not cease daily to provoke his wrath against us. And since we are much too unworthy to appear before his holy majesty, may he be pleased to receive us in the name of his beloved Son, our Lord Jesus Christ, accepting the merit of his death and passion as a recompense for all our sins, since by our own works we cannot stand before his face. And may he be pleased to enlighten us by his Holy Spirit in the true understanding of his holy word, giving us grace to handle it faithfully and to receive it in true fear and humility, so that by it we may be taught to put our trust wholly in him, to serve and honour him as we ought, to glorify his holy name in all our living and to edify our neighbour by our good example. Let us pray to him for all these things, as our Saviour and Redeemer Jesus Christ taught us to pray, saying, 'Our Father in heaven …'

PRAYER OF INTERCESSION

(*said immediately after the extempore prayer which concluded the sermon*)

And may he give this grace not only to us but to all peoples and nations of the earth, bringing those who are sadly ignorant back from their bondage to error and darkness, to the true way of salvation. To this end may he be pleased to raise up true and faithful ministers of his word, who do not seek their own advantage and ambition, but only the exaltation of his holy name and the salvation of his poor flock. May he put an end to all the sects, heresies and errors which sow the seeds of trouble and division among his people, so that we may all live together in good and brotherly concord.

May he also by his Holy Spirit guide all kings, princes and leaders who wield his sword, so that they may rule not in greed, cruelty or tyranny, nor from evil and unruly motives, but in righteousness and integrity. May we also who live under them give them all due honour and obedience, and may we peaceably and quietly serve God in all holiness and uprightness.

May he comfort all who suffer and whom he visits with various kinds of trials and crosses: those nations on which he brings pestilence, war, famine or other punishments; people beset by poverty, prison, illness, exile or any other calamity of body or affliction of spirit. May he give true patience to all until he grants them complete relief from all their ills. Especially[1] *may he have mercy on all his suffering people who are scattered and presently under the tyranny*

[1] Marginal note: 'Here particular prayer is offered for anyone who, beset by sickness, is commended to the prayers of the church.'

of Antichrist, captive to Babylon, and above all on all who endure persecution for their witness to his truth. May he strengthen them with true steadfastness, comfort them, and not permit the evildoers and ravenous wolves to vent their wrath upon them; but may he give them true constancy so that they may glory in his holy name, both in life and death. May he strengthen all his poor churches which today are in distress and are assailed for his name's sake.

May he overturn and bring to naught the counsels, devices and enterprises of his enemies, so that his glory may everywhere shine forth, and the kingdom of our Lord Jesus Christ evermore grow and advance.

We further pray that our good God may give us true perseverance in his holy faith, and may increase it in us from day to day, as we confess it now by saying, 'I believe in God the Father almighty …'

THE BLESSING OF THE PEOPLE AFTER THE SERMON:

The grace of God the Father, and the peace of our Lord Jesus Christ, through the fellowship of the Holy Spirit, remain with you forever. Amen.

INDEX OF SCRIPTURE REFERENCES

INDEX OF SUBJECTS

OTHER CALVIN TITLES TRANSLATED BY ROBERT WHITE

SERMONS ON THE BEATITUDES
Clothbound, 128 pp. ISBN: 978 0 85151 934 0

SONGS OF THE NATIVITY
Clothbound, 280pp. ISBN: 978 1 84871 010 8

A GUIDE TO CHRISTIAN LIVING
Pocket Gift Edition, 160pp. ISBN: 978 1 84871 040 5

FAITH UNFEIGNED
Clothbound, 208pp. ISBN: 978 1 84871 086 3

THE INSTITUTES OF THE CHRISTIAN RELIGION (1541 EDITION)
Clothbound, 920pp. ISBN: 978 1 84871 463 2

SERMONS ON 1 TIMOTHY
Clothbound, 864pp. ISBN: 978 1 84871 799 2

SERMONS ON 2 TIMOTHY
Clothbound, 488pp. ISBN: 978 1 84871 840 1

SERMONS ON TITUS

Clothbound, 312pp. ISBN: 978 1 84871 569 1

THE DOCTRINE OF ELECTION

Clothbound, 264pp. ISBN: 978 1 80040 265 2

IN THE POWER OF THE SPIRIT

Clothbound, 320pp. ISBN: 978 1 80040 428 1

SOME FEEDBACK FROM READERS OF CALVIN'S SERMONS

'These sermons are wonderful! Any sermon by Calvin is loaded with red meat for spiritual growth and a joy to read. I hope more of them are published. We cannot have too many Calvin sermons. They are worth reading repeatedly.'

'Calvin's pastoral tone is evident throughout. He does not preach from a position of judgment but from one of compassion, reminding his listeners that repentance is not merely an emotional response but a life-changing commitment. His emphasis on faith is equally prominent, defining it not as mere intellectual assent but as a deep trust in God's promises. His call to his congregation is clear: turn from sin, trust in Christ, and live in light of the gospel.'

BANNER *of* TRUTH

The Banner of Truth Trust originated in 1957 in London. The founders believed that much of the best literature of historic Christianity had been allowed to fall into oblivion and that, under God, its recovery could well lead not only to a strengthening of the church, but to true revival.

Interdenominational in vision, this publishing work is now international, and our lists include a number of contemporary authors, together with classics from the past. The translation of these books into many languages is encouraged.

A monthly magazine, *The Banner of Truth*, is also published, and further information about this, and all our other publications, may be found on our website, banneroftruth.org, or by contacting the offices below:

Head Office:
3 Murrayfield Road
Edinburgh
EH12 6EL
United Kingdom

Email: info@banneroftruth.co.uk

North America Office:
610 Alexander Spring Road
Carlisle, PA 17015
United States of America

Email: info@banneroftruth.org